TAKE THIS JOB
AND LOVE IT!

Also by Diane Tracy
Truth, Trust, and the Bottom Line
The First Book of Common-Sense Management
10 Steps to Empowerment

HOW TO TURN THE JOB
YOU HAVE
INTO THE JOB YOU WANT

TAKE THIS JOB
AND LOVE IT!

DIANE TRACY

BARNES
&NOBLE
BOOKS
NEW YORK

2004 Barnes & Noble Books

ISBN 0-7607-5911-1

Printed and bound in the United States of America

04 05 06 07 08 09 MC 9 8 7 6 5 4 3 2 1

Contents

Preface xiii

Acknowledgments xix

1. Refusing to Live Without Career Satisfaction 1
The Seeds of Our Discontent
A Whole New Work Environment
Getting Our Power Back
The Four-Step Career Empowerment Process

2. Achieving Success Without Losing Yourself 9
What Are the Rules?
How to Break the Rules
Getting What We Want in an Unfair System

3. Standing Up for Your Rights 33
Refusing to Be a Victim
Defending Your Rights
Respecting the Rights of Others

4. Using Positive Politics to Advance 55
Your Career
Stop Judging and Start Accepting
Define Your Career Goals and Plans
Focus on the Big Picture
You've Got to Be a Team Player
Don't Take It Personally
Build a Strong Network
Find a Mentor
Examine Your Style
Joining with Others

5. Getting a Life When Your Job Is Everything 71
High Achievers/Low Self-Esteem
Maintaining Your Self-Esteem

How Does Your Company Affect Your Self-Esteem?
Affirming Ourselves on the Job
Is Your Job Getting in the Way of Your Life?
Nurturing Ourselves on the Job
What We Need for a Balanced Life
Getting Approval from the Right Place

6. Knowing When It's Time to Move On 89
Looking at the Big Picture
You Don't Have to Like the Boss
Knowing When You've Given It Your Best
Maybe You Don't Have to Leave the Company
Weighing the Consequences
How Marketable Are You?

**7. Taking Care of Yourself When You've
Lost Your Job** 105
Don't Go It Alone
Are You Able to Ask for Help?
Putting Things in Perspective
Dealing with the Family
Facing Your Fears
Grieving the Loss
Letting Go of Anger and Resentment
Living with Your "I Don't Knows"
Nurturing Yourself During Difficult Times
You Have to Have a Plan

8. Using Plateaus to Transform Your Life 129
Plateaus—A Fact of Life
The Three Kinds of Plateaus
How Do I Know I Have Plateaued?
It's a Whole New World
The Myth About Plateauing
Obsessed with Promotion
Putting the Challenge Back in Your Job
When You've Plateaued in Life
Confronting Your Complacency

9. Turning Your Dreams into Reality 147
Dream or Die
When You Feel You Have No Dreams

Discarding the Myths
When Your Dreams Are Not Your Own
Forgiving Ourselves and Others
The Key to Our Dreams
More Ways to Discover Our Dreams
The Dream Invaders
Imaging Your Dream
Conclusion

Bibliography 167

Security is mostly a superstition. It does not exist in nature, nor do the children of men as a whole experience it. Avoiding danger is no safer in the long run than outright exposure. Life is either a daring adventure or nothing.

—*Helen Keller*

Preface

This book is not just for managers or just for workers. It is for everyone who works or who is planning to go to work. It crosses all socioeconomic lines because it addresses issues that are common to all of us as human beings—the issues of fear, power, self-esteem, and security. Whatever our job title, we all want to be treated with respect and to have self-respect. We all want to be able to put food on the table, provide for our families, and enjoy the fruits of our labors. We all want to feel that we count, that we make a difference. We all want to work in situations that enable us to reach our full potential. The principles involved in creating a career that satisfies these needs are the same for everyone, regardless of who we are or where we work. To these principles this book is devoted.

It is said that we teach what we most need to learn. And so it is with writing, at least for me. This book is as much about my own personal struggle to find career satisfaction as it is about the many companies and individuals across the country with whom I have consulted.

Before forming my own company in 1984, I worked in the corporate world for almost fifteen years. According to that world's standards, I did well. By the age of thirty, I was the youngest senior vice president in the history of a major New York City bank, earning a six-figure income. I was becoming more and more professionally accomplished, and my career was advancing at incredible speed. But there was one problem: I was miserable much of the time.

At some point, I felt like most of the characters described in this book. I was, by turns, the workaholic, the victim, the self-righteous woman who couldn't get ahead, the politician, the plateaued worker, the frustrated dreamer. Of course, I never saw myself as such, and I rarely attributed my problems and dissatisfaction to anything I did. It was always the system, poor management, company politics.

Finally I decided I just couldn't take the corporate world any longer. I was tired of fighting everyone and everything. I went into business for myself, and that is when I began to grow up.

When I first began my consulting business, I specialized in workshops and seminars that improved managerial skills. I believed that, before people could find work satisfying and before companies could reach their full potential, management would have to change. In my mind, management was the problem and the potential solution. In my attempt to fix management, to correct what I believed had been the major source of my own unhappiness, I wrote two books on management, *The First Book of Common Sense Management* and *10 Steps to Empowerment*. Both books are practical guides for helping managers create more empowered work environments.

With each book I toured the country, speaking before management groups and appearing on radio and television talk shows. Everywhere I went, I kept hearing the same thing over and over again, "I love my job but I hate the way I am managed."

An interesting thing happened almost every time I visited a radio or television station for an interview. Upon entering the door, the station personnel—everyone from the producer to the sound engineer to the on-camera personality—would tell me their own story of work woe, of how they had been treated unfairly by their boss or the company in general. Each said his or her manager could profit from reading my books on employee empowerment.

Whenever I did a call-in radio show, the telephones rang off the hook. The bitterness with which people spoke about their unfortunate work experiences was astounding. They were most critical of the heavy-handed, dictatorial manner in which their managers treated them.

The common theme of all their stories was their belief that they were powerless and that they had no personal recourse. Having been a martyr and a complainer myself, I could readily identify with these people's stories. While I felt genuine compassion for them—for many of them had been unfairly treated—as I listened, my perception of the problem slowly began to change. The thought occurred to me: "Something isn't right here. Can it all be so black and white? Is management always solely to blame, or could these people also be contributing to their own unhappiness in some way?"

While I was contemplating the question of why certain companies operate the way they do and how to change it, in my own personal life I was struggling with a similar question. My life still wasn't where I wanted it to be. I began to make changes and in the process of building a more fulfilling personal life, I gained skills and insights that also applied to creating a more satisfying career. For instance, I learned that, if I wanted to change any part of my life, I had to stop blaming others and focus on myself and on the things that I had the ability to change.

I learned that I had to stop seeing myself as helpless, assume responsibility for my life, and start taking steps toward where I wanted to be. I found that the less I judged others, the more peaceful I became and the better able I was to deal creatively with the problems and situations before me. If I wanted things to change, I had to begin with me.

I began to understand why I had been so unhappy working in the corporate world. That world may have had its injustices, and it was difficult dealing with the insidious company politics. There was a lot about that world that did not contribute to my mental and emotional health. But the larger problem was with me and my response to that world.

I saw repeating themes in my life; some of the problems I had at work were similar to problems I had in my personal life. I realized that companies and organizations are simply a microcosm of life. If you can't deal with the problems you find there, you probably can't deal with many of the problems you face in the rest of your life. For instance, I had difficulty accepting the system and the shortcomings of people at work, just as I had difficulty accepting my own shortcomings and the shortcomings of people in my personal life. The problem was not so much the people at work but my harsh judgment of them. When I left the corporate world, I took the problem with me.

With the new awareness I had about my personal life, I began to believe that, even if management didn't change, people could do certain things for themselves to create more satisfying work experiences right away. I thought that maybe people don't need new and improved management (although in many cases that would help) as much as they need to learn new skills and responses to their current work situations.

In my work as an executive coach, I've learned that people *can* change. They don't have to stay trapped in the same worn out, repetitive cycles of behavior. In fact, many of the executives with whom I have worked have inspired me to believe more in my own ability to change. Sometimes the smallest shift in our thinking and behaving can produce a significant change in our life and career.

This is not to say that it is easy. It's never easy facing ourselves and owning up to our weaknesses. In the short run it is much easier to blame other people, but in the long run we lose because we are focusing our energies outwardly on things we cannot change. The highest achievement is to master oneself and that, of course, is where the freedom lies.

I wrote *Take This Job and Love It* for a number of reasons. I wanted to validate the unease people are feeling at work. There is so much chaos and upheaval in the workplace today that many people don't even recognize the problem or how to improve things. If people can understand why things are the way they are and take responsibility for their parts in the situation, then they are in a position to do something about it.

I also wrote the book to help people manage themselves in the context of work. So many career books teach people how to interview, how to get a better job, how to strike out on their own, or how to manage people and events outside of themselves. From experience, I know that the far more difficult part of working is managing one's self—dealing with one's own emotions, perceptions, and limitations.

Perhaps most of all I wanted to give people hope and inspiration that things could be different, to help them believe that they could find satisfaction in their careers, and in many cases, in the job they are currently working.

Throughout this book, I have tried to communicate a more subtle message of compassion. Our collective work experience would improve substantially if we had more compassion, for ourselves and for the other person. Whether we are managers or workers, we are all doing the very best we can. Some of us may have greater awareness and may appear to be doing a better job, but the fact is, given what we know and our prior experiences in life, we are each doing our very best.

Many of the problems in the workplace today have to do with our judgments—the severe judgments we secretly level at ourselves and at others. We are so busy pointing the finger and blaming other people that we have little energy left for dealing creatively with our job and relationships. Some of us are so convinced that we don't deserve anything better that we don't even try. We show up to work every day in body only and mark time. We have given up the dream of having a rich, satisfying life and career. We live for the weekends and for retirement, missing all the wonderful joys that can come from working in a job that we love.

I hope this book will inspire you to resurrect your dream of finding fulfillment in your career if you don't have it. I hope it makes you just uncomfortable enough that you will choose to do something about your situation and refuse to settle for anything less than the best. And, most of all, I hope you find within these pages helpful tools for recovering your personal power so that, no matter what happens to you, you can feel safe and secure on the inside— the only place where real security resides.

For more information on seminars and services provided by Tracy Communications, contact Tracy Communications, P.O. Box 91, Wyckoff, NJ 07481, email address: dtracy@nis.net.

Diane Tracy

Acknowledgments

Writing this book has been a meaningful experience, principally because of the people in my life who have directly and indirectly played a part in bringing it to print.

First, I would like to thank my literary agent and friend, Faith Childs of the Faith Childs Literary Agency, for her relentless efforts in making sure this book found the right home. Thanks to my friend and literary mentor, Pat Golbitz, for always believing in my work, for coaching me through the various phases of this book, and for giving me my first break in the world of book writing.

My thanks to my editor and kindred spirit, Caroline Carney.

Thanks to Jeannette Kiesewetter for so patiently putting draft after draft after draft into the word processor. Thanks to my friend Andrea Zintz for her input into the manuscript and assistance with the Four-Step Career Empowerment Process. To Bud Gravette, my former mentor who taught me most of what I know about management and gave me my first real career opportunity.

I would also like to express my appreciation to Pat Roberts for the many insights she has given me which are reflected in the book. Thanks to my two close friends, JoAnn Bianca and Dawn Norris, for their constant support and inspiration, and to Sandy Gilbert, another kindred spirit who enriches my life with her wisdom and love.

To Arthur Caliandro who got me on the road to self-empowerment many years ago, without which this book would not have been written. Thanks to Mark LeBlanc, my business coach and good friend whose clarity, insight, and wisdom have helped me create a career that enriches my life. And last, to my husband, Peter Sage, thanks for showing me how to "take this *life* and love it."

1

Refusing to Live Without Career Satisfaction

The Seeds of Our Discontent

What will I do if I lose my job? Even if I keep my job, can I keep my sanity and self-esteem? How can I find a job and career that feeds my soul and, at the same time, allows me to live a balanced life? These questions haunt a new generation of workers whose expectations of job and career have changed as dramatically as the workplace in which they find themselves.

These questions, of course, aren't new. They are simply being asked in a new environment with a greater urgency to find answers. When I first wrote this book in 1994, massive layoffs and downsizing forced millions of people to rethink their lives and careers. Job security was as obsolete as the typewriter. The loss of job security was a good thing for many people. It forced them to take control of their lives and ask the question: "What do I really want to do with my life and career?"

Just as people were adjusting to the idea that they were going to have to be the CEO of their own career, we entered the most prosperous economic period in our country's history. Job security was still an issue but it was an employees' job market with unemployment at an all time low.

Just as night turns to day, the seasons come and go, the economy and job market cycle too. The return of a soft economy is causing people once again to face the issue of job security. Life is a persistent teacher. If we didn't learn the lesson the first time, the experience repeats itself until we finally get it.

Job dissatisfaction is not a new issue either. Even during the recent boom time, people were questioning whether the gilded promises offered by the corporate system were worth the sacrifice. Women, for example, have been leaving the corporate world to start their own businesses in record numbers. The Conference Board, a business research organization, recently released a survey showing that, across different age groups and income levels, U.S. workers were less satisfied with their jobs in 2000 than they were in 1995, despite the economic good times. In those five years, job satisfaction dropped from 60.9 percent to 51.2 percent among thirty-five to forty-four-year-olds, and from 57.3 percent to 46.5 percent among forty-five to fifty-four-year-olds (*BNA Daily Labor Report*, "Survey Shows Growing Job Malaise Despite Boom Times in U.S. Labor Market," October 17, 2000). Trust between employers and employees is at an all time low. Watson Wyatt Worldwide, in Bethesda, Maryland found in a study of 7,500 employees that only half trusted their senior managers. (*Wall Street Journal*, "Work and Family" column, June 21, 2000).

As concern over the economy increases, many companies and organizations appear to be demonstrating less concern for the people who work for them. Managers and employees alike are being asked to produce more and more with fewer and fewer resources. The result is a workplace that is on the verge of burnout.

The dehumanization of the workplace is escalating at a time when a human approach to management is needed more than ever—for the sake of the individual, the company, and the national economy. Job dissatisfaction always results in lost productivity. When companies fail to meet the needs of the workers, the workers have little or no desire to meet the needs of the company. When the vast majority of people in the workplace are dissatisfied with their jobs, struggling to cope with the stress stemming from ever increasing work loads and increasing mistrust, the economic implications are staggering for everyone.

The social implications of such widespread dissatisfaction and fear are also far-reaching. Job dissatisfaction is having a dramatic effect on the quality of peoples' lives and their prospects for the future. It is no small wonder that the usage of employee assistance programs has skyrocketed as well as workplace violence.

A Whole New Work Environment

One of the paradoxes is that top managers are striving harder than ever to change the cultures of their organization, to put more emphasis on the "people part" of the job, to focus on work processes instead of just the bottom line. They are facing the reality that the primary way companies gain the competitive edge today is by doing a better job of employing their human resources. Most companies today have access to the same resources, technology, and information, which means that "people" are the differentiating factor.

Yet worker dissatisfaction is a national epidemic. Why? Part of the problem is that top management wants change "overnight"; they don't understand the process involved in getting people to think and perform differently. Unknowingly, top managers often send conflicting messages to employees.

For example, they want people to be empowered; they want people throughout the organization to make more decisions. They forget that those same employees have undergone years of conditioning that said, "Just do as you are told, keep your mouth shut, and don't rock the boat." Is it any wonder, particularly considering today's job market, that many employees are reluctant to take the power that management is now giving them? Either they don't know how to make good decisions because they were never permitted to make them in the past (so that they have no experience) or they don't want to make decisions because they perceive the risk to be too high.

Another example is the movement toward self-directed work teams. For years, companies and organizations rewarded people for their individual efforts. Their salary systems and performance review systems actually encouraged people to compete and stab one another in the back. Now top management wants people to step in line, give up their aspirations of being a company "star," and embrace the team concept. While the organization's review system may still pit one person against another, top management wants people to pull together and work as a team.

These concepts of empowerment and self-directed work teams are radically changing the workplace. They are redefining work in America. Potentially, these concepts have much to offer workers and organizations, and they are long overdue.

All too often, though, we see the implementation of these concepts causing fear, chaos, and confusion. When empowerment and self-directed work teams are not properly introduced and implemented, they cause tremendous fear and anxiety among managers and workers. Managers perceive that they are being asked to give up those things that, in the past, gave them a sense of achievement, validation, and importance. In many cases, middle managers are watching their positions completely disappear as a result of self-directed work teams.

The workers are confused and bewildered, too. They are expected to think and act differently—in many respects like managers. They are being asked to perform a broader range of tasks, some for which they have no experience or training.

"What's my job?" and "Who is my real boss?" are common questions asked by workers.

Empowerment and self-directed teams, of course, are not new concepts. So much has been written and spoken about them that there's an illusion that they are successfully being implemented everywhere. In my experience as an executive coach, trainer, and speaker, I can safely say that most organizations are still in a mighty battle to transform themselves into organizations where leaders are true leaders, where people are self-managed and self-motivated, where teams are the foundation of high performance. Transformations of that magnitude take a very long time—usually two generations.

Creating an empowered work culture and implementing high-performance work teams require the people of a company to make quantum leaps in their values and beliefs. When people are asked to give up long-held values and beliefs too quickly, the result is that they resist change and fight all the harder to hold onto their old beliefs. Much of the fear and dissatisfaction in the workplace could be eliminated if management implemented change in a way that supported people in the change process and addressed their basic human fears and desires.

In many respects, the workplace has progressed in significant ways. For example, improvements such as flex hours, job sharing, telecommuting, and child care have enabled people to better integrate work and family. State-of-the-art technology has set people free so they are no longer tied to the company office. Unfortunately, there has been a price to pay for that freedom. Armed with palm pilot, laptop, cell phone, and beeper, the company has more claim to peoples' time than ever. The company owns them almost twenty-four hours a day.

The paradoxes surrounding technology are many. In the same way it frees people from the company office and binds them at the same time, it connects and disconnects people simultaneously. The speed and frequency with which people can connect with others has increased exponentially while the number of face-to-face, meaningful exchanges—the "stuff" that successful work relationships are made of—have decreased to the same degree. The flipside of the increased productivity and efficiency is greater alienation and disconnection between people—neither of which are conducive to teamwork. Synergy is lost when people aren't in right relationship with one another.

Getting Our Power Back

The continuing upheaval in the workplace is forcing more and more Americans to reexamine their past career decisions. The problem with many of us is that we turned our personal power over to the companies we work for in exchange for security, which today we realize was only an illusion. We were willing to do just about anything to please our employer so that we wouldn't have to face the grim experience of being without a job. We said what they wanted us to say, acted the way they wanted us to act, dressed the way they wanted us to dress, and in the process lost our sense of who we are. We also lost our capacity to stand on our own two feet.

Some of us still haven't recovered from the feeling of betrayal—and not just the security-bred baby boomers. Even the twenty-something dot-comers have felt betrayed—and not by the older generation but by young people their own age at the helm, promising them fortunes. When the dot-com industry went bust, employers dumped people back into the job market in ways that made traditional corporate America look kind and benevolent.

We feel panic and desperation when we feel powerless to protect and help ourselves. We ask questions like, "How can I keep my job?" or "How can I find satisfaction in the job I have?" But perhaps we need to ask the larger question first: "How can I get myself and my own power back?" "How can I feel good about myself and secure in the knowledge that, whatever happens to me, I will be able to take care of myself and my family?"

The challenges and hardships faced by companies and people today, though difficult, offer tremendous opportunity for constructive growth and change. Although the benefits to individuals may not be evident right now, in the long run many people will be well served by the experience of losing their jobs or the experience of working in an environment that fails to meet their needs. Many will once again emerge stronger than ever, more in control of their own careers and lives, clearer about what they really want. They will have a whole new set of values that will serve them and others better.

Take This Job and Love It is about taking back the power we have given to others, particularly the companies and organizations for which we work. It's about developing a whole new relationship with the companies and organizations we work for—a relationship based on autonomy and interdependence rather than paternalism and dependence.

On the following pages are stories of people who are in career crisis of some kind. They have lost their power and are in the process of taking it back. The stories are composites; they are the results of hundreds of conversations and interviews by the author with people across the country. The dilemmas are those that were the most commonly cited by the people interviewed.

First there is **Sheppard Strong**, who has achieved career success but doesn't like the person he has become in the process.

Jack Gifford is stuck in an unsatisfying job because he insists on seeing himself as a victim with no options.

Sharon McGuire has the brains and educational credentials but has failed to move up in the organization because she has no political savvy.

Judith Gordon has a problem of a different nature. Her dilemma is that she has achieved extraordinary success in her career but fears she has paid too high a price. She knows how to achieve but doesn't know how to live a healthy, balanced life.

Frank Cranston feels helpless because he can't seem to resolve his problems with his boss and doesn't know what to do about it.

Cheryl Myers has lost her job and is so paralyzed by her fears that she can't see clearly enough to take the steps she needs to help herself.

Amy Scott has reached a plateau in her life and career, feeling powerless in her ability to get off it. She feels like her life is going nowhere.

Last is **John Carmen**, who wants to make a career change but doesn't know what he wants to do. He needs a dream but doesn't know how to go about finding it.

The Four-Step Career Empowerment Process

Each chapter shows how the character uses the Four-Step Career Empowerment Process to take back his or her power and resolve the career crisis. Here is the process:

Step 1. Define the problem: If we don't know what the problem is, we can't solve it. In defining the problem we must determine which parts of the problem are caused by outside forces (such as the company, the boss, or the system) and which are caused by internal forces, by ourselves. When we separate the external causes from the internal causes, we are able to see how we have given power to sources outside ourselves. By owning and taking responsibility for the part we have played in our unhappiness, we are in a position to take back our power and make changes.

Step 2. Use the problem to create a positive vision: It is not enough to define what is wrong; we must have a vision of how we would like things to be. When we acknowledge only what we don't want or like, it is like walking backward into the future. Our vision gives us hope; it also gives our lives focus. Like the sheet of paper that burns when the magnifying glass focuses the sun's rays on it, we have power when we have focus in our lives.

Step 3. Acknowledge and accept the feelings: Our feelings are an important part of who we are and the motivating force behind our actions. It has been said that emotions are energy in motion. When we deny our feelings, we block the energy that is the source of our power. Acknowledging our feelings does not mean we have to act on them, but it helps us to accept ourselves. Self-acceptance is a prerequisite to self-empowerment.

Step 4. Make conscious choices: We get our power back and realize our vision by making choices that are carefully thought out, by making choices that meet our own approval rather than someone else's. Every time we make this type of choice, we communicate to our unconscious that we are powerful, that we can take care of ourselves. Each time we make a healthy choice, we build our self-esteem and confidence, which encourages us to make more healthy choices. We may not be able to change or control what happens around us, but we can change ourselves and how we respond.

While step 3, the feelings component, is a critical step in taking back our power, *Take This Job and Love It* focuses primarily on steps 1, 2, and 4. The "work" we do on our feelings in the process of self-empowerment is a subject unto itself and is too expansive for the scope of this book. Because it is so important, though, the list of suggested readings at the end of the book includes books on the subject.

The Four-Step Career Empowerment Process used by the characters in the book can be used by anyone in virtually any career situation. While you may not be able to readily identify with each character and his or her situation, the hope is that, by seeing the process in application, you will be able to adapt the process to resolve your own personal career crisis, creating in its place a career that provides and fosters self-esteem, self-expression, and self-fulfillment.

2 Achieving Success Without Losing Yourself

Resolve to be thyself; and know that who finds himself, loses his misery.
—*Matthew Arnold*

What price are we willing to pay for success? That is a question most of us would do well to ask ourselves early in our careers. Every great achievement, of course, requires compromise, but there is one compromise none of us can afford to make. We cannot compromise our basic values and beliefs and expect to find true satisfaction from our career successes, no matter how great they may be.

Perhaps the most difficult of all challenges in the workplace today is achieving success—in some cases simply keeping our jobs—while maintaining our sense of integrity and who we are. Doing this is a fine art that requires maturity, discipline, and risk taking. Here is a story of how one person learned to live according to his own truth after years of being the consummate company politician.

> *Sheppard Strong has achieved unusual success in his fourteen-year career. Hungry for power, money, and prestige, he has driven hard to arrive at his current position.*
>
> *The problem is that he doesn't like what he sees in the mirror every morning. It has nothing to do with the fact that he has gained a little weight and lost some of his hair. It has to do with the person he sees—the angry, manipulative, artificial person he has become since he started his grueling climb to the top.*
>
> *He simply can't bring himself to "Yes" his boss one more time when every fiber in his being is screaming "No!" If he flashes one more phony smile at one of the company's power brokers, he is certain he will become violently ill. All he wants is no more being pushed around and abused, no more bulldozing others so that he can get ahead.*

Can he make the change? Sheppard has worked hard and has obviously made more than a few sacrifices to get to his upper middle management position. Is he deluding himself to think he could possibly survive in this wolf-eat-wolf world by being honest and straightforward? Maybe he should chalk up the idea to a flight into fantasy or a moment of insanity. Maybe the pressures are getting to him and he is just cracking up.

After all, he is almost vested in the company and in line for a "mega" promotion. Jobs in his industry are not that plentiful right now either. He asks himself, "Why put it all on the line now?" Then he realizes he wouldn't, except that he feels he can't go on as he has in the past.

Somehow he has to find a way to get back some of his integrity and self-respect, and to be guided once again by his own truth without losing his job.

Sheppard's Career Empowerment Process

Defining the Problem. Sheppard's problem is that he has achieved success in the job but lost himself in the process. He has been rewarded for heeding all the spoken and unspoken rules. Unfortunately, this has led him to act in ways that are in direct conflict with what he truly feels and believes.

Creating the Positive Vision. Sheppard envisions a job and career that allows him to succeed professionally and at the same time live according to his true values.

Acknowledging and Accepting the Feelings. Sheppard must deal with his feelings of guilt, anger, and fear. He must come to terms with the way he has manipulated and misused other people and himself. He must find ways to release the anger that has built up in him over the years, as well as the anger that has resulted from having suppressed his feelings for so long. Last, he must struggle with his fear of getting fired. He must face the reality that living his own truth may mean that he has to leave the company.

Making Conscious Choices. Sheppard must first determine his real values. Although he must respect the rules, he must make all his choices on the basis of those values and their relative importance to one another.

What Are the Rules?

All systems—political, educational, religious, or familial—are governed by rules. The corporate system is no exception. By rules, we mean the dos and don'ts that the participants must honor if they are to be accepted and survive.

In most systems there are two sets of rules. One set is written down and openly acknowledged; the other is unspoken, understood, but rarely discussed by the group members. To rise to positions of power, members must abide by both sets of rules.

> **Every system is governed by rules. Those who abide by them are accepted and rewarded. Those who don't are either passed by for promotions or fired.**

Of the two sets of rules, the unspoken ones cause us greater difficulty. They are the source of much of the day-to-day stress and dissatisfaction we experience in our jobs.

Learning how to live within these rules without losing our sense of integrity is a fine art, but first we must understand these rules. Here is a sampling of the unspoken rules that exist to a lesser or greater degree in most companies:

1. The boss is always right and not to be challenged.
2. The boss is there to be served rather than to serve.
3. Appearances are more important than reality.
4. Never trust anyone but yourself.
5. Never display strong emotions or feelings.
6. If you make a mistake, you will be punished.
7. Don't be too different from your peers.
8. Always be gracious to authority figures, even when they don't deserve it.

When we abide by the unspoken rules, we are often forced to deny our true feelings and instincts. We play a role instead of expressing who we really are. One day we wake up, and, like Sheppard, we realize that something is very wrong. We feel tired and broken.

Break the Rules or Be Broken

Some of us deny our own thoughts and feelings for so long that we forget we even have them. To acknowledge the feelings would mean we would have to live in frustration and anger. To express them would mean we would have to break the rules and risk losing our jobs. Instead, we tuck our feelings away and join the ranks of the walking dead. Work becomes drudgery.

> **If the unspoken rules at our workplace are unhealthy and we abide by them to the letter, we cannot be healthy and whole ourselves. We must find a way to break the rules if we are to find fulfillment in our career and preserve our sense of integrity.**

Breaking the Rules for the Right Reasons

When we break the rules, we want to be sure that we do so for the right reasons. If we break them simply out of defiance, we may cause ourselves more problems in the long run.

> **Breaking the rules should serve the purpose of protecting ourselves and benefiting the company.**

The primary reason we abide by the unspoken rules is usually to protect our jobs. We may in fact preserve our job security, but in doing so we compromise who we are and what we believe.

When we break the rules in a mature way, we set healthy boundaries for ourselves. We don't blame or attack those who try to impose their wills on us. We simply state what we will and will not accept. The challenge is to break the rules in such a way that we don't lose our jobs in the process. (In many cases, however, losing our jobs could be the best thing that ever happened to us.)

Difficulty in Breaking the Rules

For some of us, breaking the rules will be very uncomfortable, perhaps even frightening, depending on how we view and relate to authority figures.

In some cases, our problems may be of our own making. Many of us respond to the authority figures at work in the same way we responded to our parents as children, and those responses may be totally inappropriate and unnecessary today. Let's say, for example, you grew up in a home where you were expected to be perfect. You believed that, if you made a mistake, you would be rejected. If you took this belief into your career as an adult, you would probably find yourself living with a tremendous amount of stress and anxiety. Your boss may not be nearly as harsh or demanding as the authority figure you grew up with, but you believe it to be so. You respond to your boss in the same way you responded to your parents—with fear and distrust.

Pushing the Limits

As we break the rules, we need to test the system to determine how much change in us the system will tolerate. We want to proceed gradually and cautiously so that we don't find ourselves on the street.

> **When we modify our attitudes and behaviors, the people around us will be forced to do so as well. Since most humans would rather do just about anything than change, we must evolve slowly, almost imperceptibly.**

If, for instance, you made a radical transformation all at once, the people you worked with might be shocked and may even think you were crazy. Eventually, they might even be so uncomfortable with the change in you that they decide to eliminate the source of the discomfort—namely, you.

How to Break the Rules

How we break the rules may differ from person to person, depending on our own individual needs and personality and on the system. Here are some examples of how you may break each of the unspoken rules listed earlier in the chapter. We will also see how Sheppard Strong challenged each of these rules.

Unspoken Rule 1:
The Boss Is Always Right and Not to Be Challenged

When you challenge your manager, forget about winning a point or getting her to admit she is wrong. Never challenge motives or integrity. Stick to the facts and how they relate to you. If you put yourself in an adversarial position, most likely the other person will work that much harder to defend her position, in which case you will lose. Here are more suggestions for how you can challenge your boss:

▶ Even if she deserves to be challenged at every turn, don't do so. Choose the issues you confront very carefully—only those that are really important to you.

▶ Make sure you understand your own motives. Is it to express anger or resentment? Or is it for the purpose of improving the situation?

▶ Ask yourself if the issue you're addressing is the real issue or just the symptom of a larger problem.

▶ Always make sure you have the facts to back up your point of view.

▶ Look for the common ground on which you can build. The idea is for both of you to walk away a winner.

Sheppard Challenges His Boss

Sheppard does not like confrontation. So challenging the boss is a tough one for him. As uncomfortable as it is for Sheppard to stand up for himself, he knows he must; otherwise, he feels, he may explode. It's not that Ellen is a poor boss; she just does some things that annoy him. Sheppard feels that if he can be honest with her, they can have a better relationship, and, most important, he will feel better about himself.

Sheppard has a storehouse of grievances and complaints from the past three years, but doesn't feel he should register all of them in one shot. A barrage of criticism from someone who she thought was perfectly happy in the job might leave her a bit shell-shocked.

One of his conclusions is that it would do no good to drag up old issues from the past. Even though it might help him get them off his chest, it would be counterproductive to what he is trying to achieve. Instead, he finds a friend with whom he can air the feelings as a way of letting go of those resentments.

He decides that there is one issue of major concern to him. Recently, Ellen reorganized their division and in the process took away some of his responsibilities and added others. Sheppard was not pleased with the change and didn't think it would enhance the division's ability to meet its objectives.

Sheppard carefully planned his approach. First, he made sure that he was challenging her decision for the right reasons—because he felt it was in the best interest of the division and not because his ego was hurt. When they met, he clearly explained to her his reasons for wanting to discuss the reorganization, and in doing so, he established their mutual concern for the division. Then he explained why a different type of organizational structure might enhance the division's ability to get the job done. Whenever he could, he substantiated his reasons with specific facts. Much to his surprise, Ellen listened to him and made some further changes based on some of his recommendations.

There was only one other current issue of real concern to Sheppard, which he discussed with Ellen. He decided that another list of smaller grievances was not worth mentioning.

Unspoken Rule 2:
The Boss Is There to Be Served, Not to Serve

Some people in authority sincerely believe that the people who work for them are there primarily to serve them—to meet their job requirements first. What makes matters worse is that many employees believe it too. The more bosses treat us like second-class citizens, the more we act the role. The superior and subordinate live in firmly entrenched roles in which the needs of the one with more power take precedence over the needs of the other. If the relationship is to change, someone has to break out of the role, and that someone is you. First, you must believe that you have a right to be treated as an equal, and that you have a right to have your work needs acknowledged and addressed, regardless of your position in the organization. You aren't the only one who benefits when your work needs are met. If your manager consistently ignores your needs, she is hurting not only you, but also the entire organization. Her success depends on your success and on the success of all the other people within the work group. Here are some suggestions for obtaining more support from your boss:

▶ When your manager asks you to do something and expects you to drop everything on the spot, give her a choice. Tell her you will do it but you want her to understand the consequences.

▶ If she is rarely available to you for help and for answers to questions, request an appointment in writing. Be willing to come in early or stay late.

▶ When you ask for more support, always show the benefit to her for doing so. Never criticize her for not having done so in the past.

▶ Don't whine and complain when you discuss your job needs and concerns. If you do, she will label you as a pain in the neck. Every time she sees you coming, she will want to avoid you instead of help you.

▶ Appeal to your boss's need to feel important, to be needed. If you communicate your requests in the right way, you can actually strengthen your relationship with your manager.

Sheppard Asserts Himself

Sheppard's boss, Ellen, doesn't always appreciate the demands on him. She knows his job but sometimes becomes so immersed in her own work that she fails to show him the consideration he is due. For example, she occasionally asks Sheppard to help her compile the division's monthly report at the end of the month. When she does, invariably he has a pressing deadline of his own. In the past, Sheppard would say "yes," stay late at the office to complete his own work, and then come in angry the next morning. He decided to try a new approach.

Once again, at the end of the month, Ellen asked him to help her with the report. Sheppard said "yes," provided she understood that, if he did, he wouldn't be able to meet the deadline she had assigned for the other project he was working on. This way he didn't say "no." He simply stated the facts and set his limits with her. He left the decision up to her.

In addition to setting boundaries, Sheppard becomes more assertive in asking for what he needs. For example, sometimes he becomes frustrated when he can't get in to see Ellen because she is so busy. His progress gets put on hold because he can't get the answers he needs. Ellen wants to be helpful, but there are just so many hours in the work day. To help alleviate the problem, Sheppard asks if they could make a standing appointment every Monday morning at 8 A.M.

Unspoken Rule 3:
Appearances Are More Important Than Reality

We live in a world where appearances are important, so we cannot ignore them. We can, however, make sure that the image we project is consistent with who we are and what we have to offer.

We may work in an environment where appearances and image are valued and rewarded above performance. The trouble begins when a new administration takes over the organization, a regime that decides who will stay based solely on past performance and achievement. In this case, if image isn't backed by substance, it is about as valuable as a beautifully wrapped empty box.

Here are some ways you can ensure that your image is backed by substance:

▶ Never make decisions on the basis of how it will look for you but on what is in the best interest of the company. If your decisions are not based on fact, integrity, and good judgment, they will eventually catch up with you. A decision that seemed to enhance your image at the time could turn into a nightmare.

▶ Give more than what is required. Build a reputation as being one who gets the job done and then some. You never know who is watching, and you will be noticed.

▶ When other departments and people within the organization ask for help, give it to them. Cooperate with them in such a way that you show you genuinely care. Someone in another department could be your next manager.

▶ Always look for ways to improve your value to the company. The more you increase your value to the company, the more you enhance your marketability outside the company. Stay up-to-date about what is happening in your industry. Talk to your boss and other colleagues about current trends. Read, read, read. Take seminars to improve your skills.

▶ Volunteer for special projects, particularly those with high visibility or those from which you can learn new information or skills.

▶ Be creative. Look for ways you can do the job better and more efficiently. Add value to the company and you add value to yourself.

▶ Make sure all your achievements and accomplishments are reflected in your annual performance review. If they aren't, ask your manager to add them.

▶ If you have achieved something extraordinary and you feel you haven't been properly recognized, ask why. If, for example, you feel your bonus for the year or period didn't adequately reflect your contribution, ask your manager to explain to you how the bonus was figured.

▶ If you were passed by for a promotion and you feel it was given to a person within or outside the company who was less qualified, ask your manager to tell you how the decision was made and what you could have done differently to achieve the promotion.

▶ When you are around people higher up in the organization, somehow let them know about your particularly noteworthy accomplishments.

▶ When you receive a promotion, make sure the company sends a press release to the trade press and your hometown newspaper.

These are all examples of how to improve the substance of what you bring to the company as well as your image. You should follow them for yourself, not for your boss or for anyone else. The idea is to make yourself so valuable that you can write your own ticket.

Sheppard Concentrates on Performance

Sheppard is very big on appearances, which is one of the reasons he is so exhausted all the time. He spends a lot of energy trying to figure out what will impress the big bosses. He has decided to establish a new criterion for making decisions. Instead of asking himself, "What will they think of me?" he asks, "What do I think in terms of how this will help the company?"

In the past, Sheppard has been so skilled at arranging appearances that he hasn't always done the job as he should. He does an outstanding job of putting together proposals and plans for high-visibility projects, but then he passes most of the work on to others and fails to follow up. He has decided to put an end to that, too.

He's going to start pulling his share and paying more attention to detail. He intends to begin with the upcoming product introduction. This time he is going to work more closely with all the other departments involved so that they can coordinate their efforts, something that has always been a problem in the past. Instead of letting them work in a vacuum, he is going to take more of a leadership role. When they ask him for help and information, he's not going to brush them off as though they are a bother. One small way he is going to begin is by returning their phone calls.

Sheppard also decides to stop promoting himself so much. In the past, when he accomplished something, everyone knew it. Around the company, he's known for being a big talker. His company is threatened with a takeover; so he has more reasons to improve his performance than just his integrity and self-esteem. If he wants to keep his job, he knows he better devote more time to producing and less to talking about what he has done or plans to do.

Unspoken Rule 4:
Never Trust Anyone But Yourself

When we don't trust anyone but ourselves, we end up in isolation. It is tough to find satisfaction at work when we live behind a wall of defenses, always watching to see who might "do us in" next. Naturally we can't trust everyone, but surely we can find a few souls within the organization who are worthy of our trust. We need people with whom we can let down the façade and be ourselves. Otherwise, keeping up the guard and the front is just too exhausting. Here are a few suggestions for establishing trusting relationships within the organization.

▶ Try to establish one or two relationships outside your department. Develop a friendship with someone who can be objective with you about your situation and with whom you can talk about things other than work.

▶ In selecting your trusted friends, watch with whom they work closely, eat lunch, and mingle at company functions. Their associates will tell you a lot about them.

▶ As you build a trusting relationship, reveal yourself gradually. Don't tell your life story over your first lunch—or even the second.

▶ Use your friendships as a way to escape the pressures and strains of your job. When you feel you are about to explode, take time out with a friend and have a good laugh or a good cry, whichever makes you feel better.

▶ When you find those you can trust, don't use them as a dumping ground. Let off steam when you need to, but don't let criticism of others be the basis of your relationships.

▶ Remember that every relationship entails a certain amount of risk. Taking risks and being disappointed every now and then is better than living in total isolation.

▶ Trust the people who report to you when the trust is earned. Trust begets trust.

Sheppard Learns to Trust

Sheppard trusts no one, partly because he himself is not totally trustworthy. In his personal life, Sheppard is getting professional help with some of his problems; he realizes his life is not working and is willing to do something about it. He is especially weary of the loneliness and isolation.

One of the ways he is trying to be more trusting is by being more open at work, by reaching out to other people. Realizing that his work environment is not a place that breeds trust, he's proceeding cautiously.

There is a fellow named Art in another department who seems like a nice guy. He more or less minds his own business but has always been very supportive of Sheppard when they work on projects together. He has asked Sheppard to play golf with him on a few occasions.

Although Sheppard isn't skilled at forming close relationships, he is trying. When things at work become too stressful, instead of working that much harder to avoid the feelings, as he has done in the past, he takes a break and visits Art.

Telling Art how he feels is a big risk for Sheppard. At first, it felt very uncomfortable, and then it became such a source of relief that Sheppard began to go to the other extreme. All he did when he visited Art was complain and let off steam. Eventually, his periodic visits stopped helping and sometimes even made him feel worse.

Through the help he was receiving in his personal life, Sheppard learned that trust didn't mean complete disclosure at all times, nor did it mean using one's friends to dump feelings. Sheppard is learning to have healthy, trusting relationships at *work with a select few and is reaping the rewards. He has a much greater sense of well-being.*

Unspoken Rule 5:
The Expression of Strong Feelings and Emotions Is Unacceptable

One of the primary ways we lose ourselves at work is by denying our feelings. We conceal them rather than pay the consequences of expressing them. And then they come out sideways, in all kinds of ways that are destructive to ourselves and others.

If we are to survive as healthy, well-adjusted persons at work, we must find ways to express the feelings that go with being human.

The problem is that we are rewarded for being "human doings," not for being human beings. We are expected to operate from our intellect, not from our feelings. Here are some suggestions for maintaining your humanity and sanity on the job:

- ▶ Laugh. It will be good for your soul and everyone else's. It's also good for your health. Even if no one else laughs, you still can. Others may just find you a breath of fresh air in a stodgy, stale environment.
- ▶ If you manage people, use humor to break the tension and relax them. Let them know you are human.
- ▶ If you are truly excited about something, let people know by expressing genuine joy and excitement. Let it show in your face, in your body language, and in your tone of voice—not just in your words.
- ▶ When you are angry, tell the object of your anger how you feel. Telling people that you are angry to their faces is much more healthy than smiling as though all is well and finding subtle underhanded ways to sabotage them behind their back.
- ▶ When you like and admire a person, don't be afraid to say so—and that includes your manager. It's highly unlikely that you will be rejected for giving persons what most of them want more than anything—acceptance and validation. If your comment is sincere, you will probably make a friend and ally.
- ▶ Listen to your feelings. If you work only from your head, you will get very, very tired, and you will second-guess

yourself. When we ignore our intuitive sense, we miss out on valuable information.

▶ When someone else is having a tough time, whether work-related or personal, don't be afraid to show compassion. As the saying goes, "Nothing is so strong as gentleness, nothing so gentle as real strength."

▶ If you are having a really tough day, as we all do from time to time, don't fake cheerfulness. You will only make yourself feel worse. Give yourself permission to feel rotten every now and then. But do it without lashing out at others and being a spoil sport.

▶ Be truthful but tactful. Don't exaggerate the positive when your genuine feeling is that something is actually mediocre or poor.

▶ Remind yourself that feelings aren't good or bad. They just are. It's what we do with them that counts.

Sheppard Expresses His Feelings

Sheppard's demeanor at work is almost always the same. The permanent plastic smile on his face, coupled with a constant flow of "rah, rah, everything is terrific" rhetoric, belies what is really going on inside him. He can be furious and you would never know, except for those few perceptive people who can see beyond the mask. His feelings never seem to match what he says and does, which is one of the reasons his peers and the people who work for him don't trust him. Something just isn't "right."

Sometimes, Sheppard doesn't know what he is feeling himself, he is so accustomed to shutting off his feelings. Rather than risk looking unprofessional and out of control, Sheppard takes on a persona that he feels will keep him safe and allow him to be accepted.

Sheppard received acceptance from his company for always remaining in strict control, but he paid a high price for it. He felt he had betrayed himself because he acted like a phony so much of the time.

Lately Sheppard has begun to pay more attention to his feelings and is expressing them. When he is angry with his boss, Ellen, he tells her so. He has learned to express his anger at her in a way that doesn't place blame or attack; he simply states how he feels.

Because of her busy schedule, Ellen is constantly postponing their 8 A.M. appointments. Finally, one day he said, "Ellen, when you constantly postpone our scheduled meetings, I feel angry and frustrated. I feel that I and my work are very low on your priority list." Ellen had no idea he felt that way, and from then on she made a greater effort to keep her appointments with Sheppard.

Sheppard also expresses his feelings more to the people who work for him. He makes a conscious effort to acknowledge their individual efforts and, when appropriate, tells them how much he appreciates them. If he knows one of his people is going through a difficult time or in the middle of a personal crisis, he finds ways to let them know he empathizes with them. He might, for example, give them the afternoon off or just ask how they are doing.

In his decision making, Sheppard also tries to listen more to his intuitive sense. Instead of always working from his head, he has begun to listen more to his gut. To his surprise, when he does, he finds he is usually right.

Recently, for example, he interviewed a number of people for a middle-management position. One of the candidates didn't have as many credentials as the others, but something told him to hire the person. A few months later, he was at a trade meeting talking with some of his peers in other companies. The candidate's name came up in conversation. Sheppard learned some things about the person in the course of conversation that confirmed his feelings.

Unspoken Rule 6:
If You Make a Mistake, You Will Be Punished

Some of us rarely make a mistake because we never take any risks or because we drive ourselves crazy trying to be perfect. We are like ships that stay safely in harbor and never go out to sea; as a result, we never reach our full potential.

In the workplace, permission to make mistakes must come from your manager and from you.

Let's start with you, since that's the one you can change. Many of us don't take risks and make mistakes because we are too tough on ourselves. We have all kinds of ideas about what it means to make an error or to fail. We make incorrect assumptions about what will happen to us if we do. Here are some suggestions for giving yourself permission to be less than perfect:

▶ Tell yourself that failure goes hand in hand with great success. Just look at the great leaders of the world. Their lives are studded with failures as well as successes.

▶ Remember that you are not your achievements or your failures. Neither has anything to do with your worth as a person.

▶ Look at your mistakes as opportunities to learn. Ask your boss for advice on how to avoid making the mistake again. If you never fell down as a child, you would have never learned to walk.

▶ If you are afraid to take a risk for fear of failing, talk it out with a friend. Confront your worst fears—the things that could happen if you make a mistake but probably never will.

▶ If you do make a mistake, keep it in its proper perspective by reminding yourself of all the good things you have done.

▶ Build a reputation for yourself as being professional. People will look at your mistakes differently if they know you usually meet high standards. It is the careless errors that reflect most poorly on us.

▶ If you manage people, offer them the same permission to make mistakes that you desire for yourself.

▶ When you consider taking on a challenge, remind yourself what you might miss if you don't take it.

▶ Carefully plan the risks you take. Weigh the potential cost of failure against the potential benefits.

As you occasionally make the mistakes that go with risk taking, you will want to find ways to protect yourself. Here are some things you can do to minimize the negative consequences of your mistakes:

▶ When you have made a mistake, be the first to let your boss know. It may be possible to correct it before serious damage results. Covering up—or lying about mistakes—is unprofessional and your boss will regard you accordingly. In the end, the consequences could be worse.

▶ When you have made a mistake, tell your manager what you have done and what you plan to do to correct it. Don't pass the problem on to her and expect her to solve it for you.

▶ If you're unsure about how to answer a question or solve a problem, ask for help. Don't try to handle everything on your own. Extreme independence can be as harmful as overdependence.

Sheppard Takes a Risk

Sheppard is a highly creative person who has contributed only a small fraction of what he is capable. He has been unwilling to take the risks involved in pursuing his own good ideas. Terrified of failure, Sheppard pursues only those activities and projects that he is relatively certain will succeed.

Through the years, a quiet little voice within has nagged him. It tells him that he is missing real satisfaction and fulfillment in his work, that he is failing to reach his full potential because he won't take risks. He decides to confront his fear of failure and begins to take small risks. At meetings, for example, if he has a thought or opinion that is totally different from everyone else's, he throws it out to the group to consider its merit. Sheppard is discovering, and so is everyone else, that he has some unique talents that haven't been used in the past.

Sheppard is also beginning to "think bigger." Instead of operating strictly within the parameters of his job description, he is pursuing some of the ideas that in the past he kept on the shelf. As a result, executive management has been giving him more special projects.

Sheppard has always been skilled at protecting himself, but now that he is taking more risks, he is having to do so in different ways. He is staying in closer contact with Ellen so that she can guide him through some of the tricky spots. As a result, Sheppard and Ellen have come to trust each other, to the benefit of them both.

Unspoken Rule 7:
Don't Be Too Different from Your Peers

A system that doesn't allow us to take risks usually doesn't allow us to be different from the other members of the group, whether better or worse. If we want to be accepted, we must conform to a strict norm.

This rule, like the others, is usually based in fear. Conformity is simply another word for control. We believe that, if we follow the organization's prescription for dress, behavior, and performance, we can control what happens to us. We believe that, if we stick to our dark suits and neat haircuts, we can ensure our job security.

Naturally, in any group we will have to conform to some degree. Groups can't function without rules and the willingness of the members to abide by the rules. Problems occur when the rules are so strict and rigid that we lose our individuality. If, for example, we take on a persona that is not ours—if we speak in ways that are unnatural to us and say things we don't mean—the group loses as well as the individual. It is our differences, not our similarities, that add richness to the group.

Regardless of what the other members of the group do, we must find ways to express our own uniqueness at work, even if it is in small ways. Here are some suggestions:

▶ Make a list of the ways you conform to the group—the big and small things you feel you must do to be accepted. Check off the ones that cause you the most difficulty. For each of the items checked, ask yourself how important it is to your career. Ask yourself what would happen if you failed to conform on these points.

▶ Look at your wardrobe. Do you like the way you dress? Do you look just like the person in the office or at the desk next to you? Does your dress express who you are?

If you are unhappy with your answers and you would like to change your appearance, find out what constitutes professional dress in the workplace. Read books on image and dress; look at pictures of professional people in business and government; spend an hour or two with an image consultant. With that information in mind, pick out clothes for work that you like, instead of those that look like everyone else's. Who knows, you may become a trendsetter!

If you do depart from the company's unspoken dress code, do so carefully. Don't be too flashy. Make sure you look professional and well groomed, and always follow the company's written dress code.

Your new look should draw attention because you look "smart," distinctive, and stylish rather than different or weird.

▶ If you detest going to company social functions such as cocktail parties and long boring dinners, find ways to satisfy your obligation without taxing yourself to the limit. First ask yourself which ones you can say "no" to. Some of them may be totally unnecessary and will not add one thing to your career advancement. Before you leave, make sure you see the people who need to know you are there.

▶ If one or more of your peers invites you to play tennis and you don't enjoy the sport, it's permissible to decline. You'll be doing yourself and probably everyone else a favor. Reciprocate by asking people to participate in sports or other activities that you both enjoy.

▶ If you travel with people who regularly participate in long cocktail hours and dinners that you don't especially enjoy, go for part of the evening and then do what you want to do. Or if you want to go to a play or some other local event, tell the group what you plan to do and that you will be happy to arrange for tickets for everyone.

▶ Be decisive. If your boss asks you what kind of food you like, tell him. That's why he asked. Even if you are a subordinate, you have a right to likes and dislikes.

▶ When it comes to performance, always try to distinguish yourself through excellence, but don't brag about successes in front of your peers. Find subtle ways to let the big bosses know when you have achieved something noteworthy.

▶ If you are a star performer, work extra hard at being a team player. Stars are often a threat to other people, particularly those who are insecure. You can diffuse their fear and gain acceptance by showing them that they can only benefit by being associated with you. For example, if you spearhead a project involving a lot of other people, share the glory when it's a success. Let them take some of the spotlight. Build them up instead of touting your own accomplishments. You'll have everything to gain and nothing to lose by doing so.

▶ If you are a star performer, don't be so obsessive that you forget your colleagues in the process. Take a few minutes every now and then to sit down with one of your peers and shoot the breeze. Talk about things that are totally unrelated to work.

Sheppard Takes More Risks

Sometimes Sheppard feels like a clone who has been processed and given the company's seal of approval for looking, acting, and talking just like every other male manager in the organization.

Sheppard knows that he has to conform to some degree, the question is, "How much?" He dislikes three things most about working at his company. First, he is tired of laughing in unison with everyone else when the bosses tell jokes or make comments that aren't funny. Second, he despises the clothes he has to wear. When he looks at the men's attire, including his own, a sick feeling comes over him. They look like seventh graders trying to "fit in" by wearing almost identical clothes, even down to the brand label. And they look uncomfortable. Last, he can't stand going to the many company social functions. People stand around in their "uniforms" trying to fake having a good time while they watch everything they say and do carefully for fear they will make a poor impression on the bosses.

Sheppard analyzes each issue carefully to see if there is some way he can break away from the norm without hurting himself professionally. On the subject of laughing at the jokes that aren't funny, he's come to the conclusion that sometimes it is very difficult, particularly in small groups, not to laugh. He can, however, stop laughing on cue at every poor joke or comment intended to be funny just so that he can be like everyone else. From now on, he is going to laugh at what he thinks is funny. If it isn't humorous but he feels he must respond, he will smile instead of automatically going into his phony laughter.

On the issue of dress and appearance, he decides there isn't a lot he can do, except to take some small liberties and change his attitude. Most of the people in positions of authority in his company wear their hair extremely short and dress very conservatively—black, blue, or gray suits and solid colored shirts.

One of the things he decides to do is let his hair grow about a quarter inch. He won't look as though he just came out of the

Army. It's a small thing, but will help give him some sense of freedom in how he looks.

He sticks with the dark suits and solid colored shirts but plans to add some distinction by wearing brightly colored ties. Most important, he changes his attitude, which helps him feel better about looking like everyone else. A lot of professions require a uniform of sorts, and corporate America happens to be one of them. Sheppard has decided to accept the fact and express himself more through his leisure clothes to compensate for having to wear clothes he doesn't like at work.

The social functions are another matter. In the past, Sheppard has gone to everything, not because he liked them but because he believed it was expected. He looked at his datebook for the last year to see how many and what kinds of functions he had attended. To his surprise, he found that some of them had been totally unnecessary—like the company picnic, where there were so many people he would not have been missed.

Sheppard developed a list of questions for determining which ones he would go to in the future:

- Who is having the function and who will be there?
- Will there be someone at the function with whom 1 need to establish a better relationship in order to get the job done?
- Have any events in the company taken place, or may they take place, such as a merger or office move, that may affect my career? If so, could my future be enhanced in any way by attending?

Sheppard also elects to make better use of the time he spends at company social functions. He decides to seek out the people who can make a difference in his career and make himself better known to them. He will also use these affairs as a way of building his relationships with his peers and with the people who report to him.

Unspoken Rule 8:
Always Be Gracious and Polite to Authority Figures, Even If They Don't Deserve It

One of the ways we demean ourselves at work is by fawning over the people in power. We know it's hypocritical to deny our true feelings to secure our job or gain a better position. It is no wonder we don't like the person we see in the mirror. So much of what we think we have to do at work to get ahead amounts to phoniness.

Here are some suggestions for how you can break this rule without being rude or offensive:

▶ Remind yourself that the people in authority are only people. The only power they have over you is the power you give them. The bottom line is that you can always leave.

▶ Treat the people in power with the same respect you would give to a lower-level person in the organization or to your next door neighbor, provided they have earned it.

▶ Refuse to be bullied, belittled, or intimidated by anyone, regardless of their title or position. You don't have to fly off the handle, make a scene, or get emotional. All you have to do is stand up for yourself. The idea is to protect yourself without placing blame on the other person.

▶ If you do act hypocritically toward a person in authority, which may be necessary at times, make a conscious choice to do so. Don't automatically revert to your people-pleasing role.

▶ Remember that patronizing behavior and insincerity can work against you with some people, particularly those who are able to see through appearances. Those who are secure about themselves, who don't need to be reminded of their power, will be turned off.

Sheppard Refuses to Take Abuse

Sheppard intensely dislikes some people in high-level positions within the organization. One in particular has mistreated Sheppard repeatedly. This man hasn't necessarily singled Sheppard out; he regularly intimidates people in his own division as well as others as a way of asserting his power.

Despite the obnoxious behavior of this manager, Sheppard, like everyone else, goes out of his way to be friendly and accommodating to him, even when he is on one of his rampages. In keeping with his efforts to be truer to himself, Sheppard draws the line with this character. Recently, he stormed into Sheppard's office demanding to be told how and why a certain error was made. In a loud, screaming voice he

*called Sheppard and his people a bunch of "incompetents."
What was worse, the error wasn't even made by Sheppard's
department.*

*Sheppard's reply to him went something like this: "I under-
stand you're upset about this problem. If you want me to help
you, I must ask you to stop screaming at me and calling me and
my staff names. If we did in fact make the error, I will accept
full responsibility for it and do whatever 1 can to correct it.
However, I cannot permit you to speak to me in this way. If you
clearly define the problem for me and give me whatever facts
you have, I will investigate it for you."*

*Sheppard had to take a very deep breath before he responded
in this way, but when it was over he felt a strange sense of relief
and was very proud of himself. He had defended himself as he
would have defended a member of his family or a close friend.
The interesting thing was that the person backed off on that
occasion and never tried to intimidate Sheppard again.*

*Sheppard has changed the way he relates to authority figures
within the company in general, whether they are abusive or
not. Instead of doing cartwheels in their presence and trying to
figure out what they want to hear, he tries to act naturally. It
was hard at first because he was so accustomed to impressing
people, instead of just being himself. Whenever he is in their
presence, he reminds himself that they are people like him, that
he has just as much worth as a person. They just happen to be
in higher positions.*

Getting What We Want in an Unfair System

Some of the characteristics of the corporate system that cause us
stress and dissatisfaction are rigidity, silence, denial, and isolation.
We must obey the rules; we must not express ourselves candidly;
we must deny the way things are, such as how belittled we feel by
management. The result is that we are alienated from ourselves and
isolated from one another.

> **What is needed is a system that encourages flexibility,
> expression, acceptance, and caring for one another.**

What we need and what we get are often two different things.
Much of what we experience in the workplace is not fair; we

shouldn't have to work in an environment that violates our integrity and self-esteem. But life itself is not always fair. The key is learning how to get our needs met in an unfair system. We do that neither by totally giving ourselves over to the system nor by fighting the system and proving that we are "right." We do it by understanding it, accepting it for what it is, and finding creative ways to work within it.

3 Standing Up for Your Rights

> *Man must cease attributing his problems to his environment, and learn again to exercise his will—his personal responsibilities.*
> —*Albert Schweitzer*

Most of us, if we work long enough, will at some time find ourselves in a job that causes us constant frustration and grief. While we often attribute our problems to personality conflicts, most of the problems stem from not having our work needs met. We aren't quite sure what our job is or how we are supposed to do it; we don't get enough information, feedback, or recognition; or we don't feel we can trust our manager.

These unmet work needs, however, are only one part of the problem. Our response to the situation is the other. Instead of taking responsibility for getting our needs met, we rant and rave to people who can't do anything about the problem. We play the victim's role and bemoan our sad plight. In the following story, we see how the character learned to stop blaming others for his misery and do something about his unsatisfying situation.

Jack Gifford is tired. He is tired of not being able to get his job done as he knows it should be. He is tired of the politics. He's tired of feeling like Mount St. Helen's every night when he comes home. Most of all, he's tired of feeling tired. And his family is getting tired of him.

Jack feels that many things are wrong at work, but when he tries to tell someone he can't seem to put it into words. He feels like a gerbil on a runaway treadmill in a giant steel cage. The only thing getting exercised is his patience. There's duplication of effort between his job and someone else's in another department. He doesn't have the staff he needs, nor does he have the authority to hire them. He sometimes gets called on the carpet for not meeting his boss's expectations. The only time he gets any feedback or recognition is when he has done something wrong.

Jack has climbed onto the pity pot. At night when he goes home, it is, "Poor me, poor me, pour me another drink." He is thinking about jumping ship and going to the competition, but when he talks to his friends they all seem to be sailing in the same murky waters. The worst part is how he feels about himself. His self-esteem is in need of a major overhaul.

Jack tells himself that, if he could just do something about his situation, he would feel better—but he feels trapped with no place to go. Without a college degree, he figures finding another job at the same pay would be tough. He has a mortgage to pay and a family to support. Jack is sick of hearing himself complain. He knows he needs to do something about his situation—but what?

Jack's Career Empowerment Process

Defining the Problem. Jack's problem is that he sees himself as a victim with few or no alternatives. He has convinced himself that his situation is hopeless. He continues to complain instead of taking action.

Creating the Vision. Jack envisions himself working in a job that supports him in his efforts to give his best effort to the company. Most important, he wants to work in a company that is managed by sound management principles—a company that clearly defines the expectations, gives him the resources to meet those expectations, and rewards him for doing so.

Acknowledging and Accepting the Feelings. Someone once said that whining and complaining are nothing more than anger coming through a small keyhole. Jack must deal with his feelings of anger over not getting his work needs met. He must also come to terms with his feelings of low self esteem and lack of self-confidence.

Making Conscious Choices. Jack must make choices that will get him out of the victim role. Instead of complaining, he must take actions which will enable him to get more of his work needs met. If he can't get them met to his satisfaction in his current situation, he must choose to either lower his expectations or move on.

Refusing to Be a Victim

Some of us are masters at playing the victim's role. Not all victims simply sit around and feel sorry for themselves; many are hard-working, perfectionistic high achievers, better known as martyrs. We live in a web of self-pity and resentment that keeps us stuck. We believe the problem is entirely with other people, and we think someone else should fix it.

We may, in fact, have been victimized and have a right to our feelings of anger and resentment. However, when we stay stuck in the past, reliving old hurts, constantly resurrecting every injustice ever done to us, we punish ourselves. We spend our energies reliving the past instead of taking steps to free ourselves of situations that may not be good for us.

When we focus on what others have done to us, we also fail to look at the part we may have played in the situation. By focusing on the other person, we abdicate our responsibility to ourselves to be the best person we can be. How can we, when we are constantly pointing the finger at others and trying to control them?

The real question is whether we will continue to allow ourselves to be treated unjustly. As one wise person put it, there are no victims, only willing volunteers (except, of course, in the case of children). Our power comes from realizing that we have options and that we can exercise those options. We give our power away when we allow ourselves to be immobilized by fear, anger, and resentment.

Why would anyone want to remain a victim? Surely there must be some payoff for doing so. The most common reason is that, when we see ourselves in that light, we don't have to take responsibility for our well-being. Instead we spend our energies complaining and looking for sympathy from others. Some remain the "poor mistreated ones" because they have a need to be abused; the abuse gives credibility and validation to the way they feel about themselves and what they feel they deserve.

> **The first step in finding a more satisfying job or career is to refuse to see ourselves as victims.**

What's Your Victim Quotient?

Most of us would just as soon not see our "warts." We would rather live in delusion about who we are and what we look like to the outside world. Here is a short quiz for the brave at heart who are willing to do anything to get out of their unhappy job situation, even if it means looking at themselves.

	Yes	No
1. Are you constantly projecting what's going to happen to you and your job?	❏	❏
2. Do you worry a lot about your job situation?	❏	❏
3. Do you often feel sorry for yourself because of your job situation?	❏	❏
4. Do you try to manipulate and control others around you?	❏	❏
5. Do you dramatize events at work and blow them out of proportion?	❏	❏
6. Are you in constant search of approval at work?	❏	❏
7. Do you resent your boss and/or the people with whom you work?	❏	❏
8. Do you find yourself whining and complaining about all the things that are wrong at work?	❏	❏
9. Do you blame your boss or other people at work for your unhappiness?	❏	❏
10. Do you constantly remind yourself and/or others how much you are sacrificing for the company?	❏	❏

If you answered "yes" to:
0–2 questions: You're in pretty good shape; you are human.
3–5 questions: You are bordering on victimhood.
5–10 questions: You are a hard core victim.

Getting Out of the Victim Role

If you scored high on the victim scale, you may be wondering how you can go about getting rid of the big V, which unknowingly you have been wearing across your forehead. How can you go about changing the behaviors that are keeping you stuck?

First, you need to understand that you have certain rights on the job. You need to know what they are and assume responsibility for them by standing up for yourself in a mature way.

Some of us have worked at the hands of poor managers for so long that we don't even know we have rights. Out of fear we lay down and let others walk over us. Or we let others mistreat us and then we get back at them in subtle, underhanded ways that are every bit as destructive.

> **To get out of the victim role, you must understand that you have rights and assume responsibility for those rights by standing up for yourself.**

Your Bill of Rights

When we talk about rights on the job, we are talking about more than just those protected by the employment and labor laws. We are talking about the rights you have as a person to work in an environment that gives you a sense of your own personal power, about your right to work in an environment that supports you in your efforts instead of constantly working against you, about your right to be treated with respect and dignity.

The problem is that our rights all too often are not even acknowledged, much less honored. Some managers who are of the "we/they" mentality believe that, if people are too happy, they will take advantage of management and won't do the job.

Bill of Rights

1. The right to have your responsibilities clearly defined.
2. The right to have enough authority to fulfill your responsibilities.
3. The right to know the standards and to be encouraged to achieve excellence.
4. The right to receive the training needed to meet the job standards.
5. The right to receive the knowledge and information you need to do the job.
6. The right to receive feedback.
7. The right to be recognized.
8. The right to be trusted when it is earned.
9. The right to make mistakes.
10. The right to be treated with respect.

Other managers, probably the majority, fail to meet our needs and honor our rights, not out of any mistrust or ill will, but out of ignorance. They were never taught the principles and fundamentals of management that are essential to being an effective leader. Regardless of the reason, the consequences to us are the same.

> **Only when your rights are honored are you able to give your best to the company and to achieve a sense of personal satisfaction in your career.**

The rights listed in the box at the top of this page are the foundation of empowerment. Empowerment is simply being able to achieve our objectives and reach our potential. When these rights are honored, we are able to give our best to the job.

When these rights are not honored, we live with the pain of ambiguity. If we don't know what we are supposed to do, if we don't know the basis on which we will be evaluated or how well we are doing, we spend much of our time and energy trying to figure things out. We spend our time trying to "stay safe" and protecting our jobs instead of doing the jobs.

Defending Your Rights

Since the workplace is filled with managers either who don't know how or who have no interest in honoring your rights, it is up to you to defend them. Granted, you shouldn't have to ask for the things that are rightfully yours, but life is rarely as it should be.

> **The sooner we accept the injustices of the system and take responsibility for ourselves, the better off we will be.**

What do you do if your rights are being violated? Do you stage a work strike? Write a letter to the chairman? Point out to the boss that his management skills leave something to be desired? These are actions to avoid, unless we harbor a secret desire to be fired.

The first step is to clearly define the problems. The next is to let your concerns be known to the person who can do something about them. Problems can't be resolved if your boss doesn't know they exist. Like spouses who become hurt and angry because their partners can't read their minds, who end up in the divorce court without even knowing why, we sometimes create unnecessary conflicts with our employers simply because we don't communicate our feelings to them.

On the following pages is a more detailed description of your rights, along with a list of questions to help you evaluate your own job situation. Following the questions, we'll show you how our character, Jack Gifford, learned to stop playing the victim by asserting his own work needs.

The Right to Have Your Responsibilities Clearly Defined

You can neither enjoy your job nor achieve success if you don't have a clear understanding of your responsibilities. A vague, general idea simply won't do.

Without a clear definition of your responsibilities, you end up playing the guessing game, doing what you think you are supposed to do—which may be different from what your boss expects.

Do You Have a Clear Understanding of Your Responsibilities?

	Yes	No
1. Are you confident that you know what your job is most of the time?	❏	❏
2. If you are a member of a self-directed work team, does the team regularly communicate your responsibilities to you?	❏	❏
3. Do you understand how your job relates to the department's/team's goals and objectives?	❏	❏
4. Does your manager/team prioritize your responsibilities as plans change?	❏	❏
5. Do you feel a sense of ownership and pride in the responsibilities that have been assigned to you?	❏	❏
6. Is the work in your area organized in such a way that there is little or no duplication?	❏	❏
7. Do you and your fellow team members understand each others' responsibilities?	❏	❏

If you answered "no" to more than one or two questions, you probably spend a fair amount of time trying to figure out what you are supposed to do. You need to have your responsibilities clarified.

Jack Asks for Clarification

When Jack took on his current position, it had been newly created. At that time, he wasn't entirely sure what it entailed; all he knew was it was an increase in responsibility and pay.

In the beginning Jack felt he was floundering but chalked it up to the adjustment that goes with any new job. He has been in the job a year now and is still in doubt about his responsibilities. In the past year, he seems to have jumped from one project to another with no rhyme or reason.

His job is the by-product of a company-wide reorganization. It was formed by combining two positions into one. One of the departments believes their former responsibilities are still theirs; so he finds himself constantly duplicating the work of the other department, and vice versa.

Jack decides to talk to his boss about his problem. He tells him he has some concerns as to whether he is concentrating on the right activities. Since he doesn't have a written job description, that's the first thing he asks for, and he offers to assist in writing it. Jack asks his boss if they could meet periodically to discuss what his priorities should be for a given time frame.

He makes a conscious decision to stop worrying about appearing stupid when he is uncertain about what he should be doing. Instead, he asks.

The Right to Have Enough Authority to Fulfill Your Responsibilities

If you are to fulfill your responsibilities and achieve success, you must be given the authority to do so. The amount of decision making delegated to you will directly affect the amount of responsibility you are able to fulfill. Regardless of your talents, skills and desire, if you don't have the authority, you are powerless to get the job done. You're like a steamboat without steam.

Do You Have Enough Authority to Fulfill Your Responsibilities?

	Yes	No
1. Do you have authority equal to your responsibilities?	❑	❑
2. Were you told before you were hired how much authority you would have?	❑	❑
3. Does your job description clearly define your authority levels?	❑	❑
4. When your manager/team delegates large tasks to you, are the boundaries of your authority clarified?	❑	❑

5. Do the people who work with you understand your ❑ ❑
   authority levels?
6. Do you feel confident most of the time that you ❑ ❑
   aren't overstepping your bounds or failing to
   do enough?
7. Have your authority levels increased over time as ❑ ❑
   you've demonstrated your ability to take on more
   decision-making?

If you answered "no" to more than one or two questions, you are probably frustrated in your ability to get your job done. You need to convince your boss that you need more authority—authority equal to your responsibility.

Jack Asks for More Authority

"I have the responsibility but I don't have the authority" is a phrase often repeated by Jack. He is short three people but doesn't have the freedom to hire them. Consequently, morale is low and productivity is down in his area. He spends more time doing the work himself rather than managing. If the work doesn't get done, his neck is on the line.

Jack and his staff have a substantial amount of contact with customers. When customers complain, Jack doesn't have the authority to correct problems on the spot, except on very minor issues, and that makes them even more irate.

Tired of feeling stonewalled at every turn, Jack decides to take action. First, he figures out exactly how much authority he needs and why, and then he puts his request and reasons in a memo to his boss. To justify his request, he writes down specific instances over the last six months when he could have been more effective and productive if he had been given adequate authority.

He uses as an example the enraged customer who finally took his business elsewhere because he had been bounced around from person to person, none of whom had the decision-making power to resolve his problem. That one small incident cost the company thousands of dollars in lost business.

Jack is aware his boss likes to hold onto power, so he gives adequate reasons why he can handle the additional authority. He even offers to keep his boss updated on a more frequent basis

*until he is comfortable that Jack is capable of making more deci-
sions. Subtly, he reminds his boss that the more efficiently and
decisively he can act, the better the boss will look to his bosses.*

The Right to Know the Standards and to Be Encouraged to Achieve Excellence

You can't meet your manager's expectations if you don't know
the standards. And you can't experience a sense of pride in your
work if you are not asked to strive for excellence.

Standards or guidelines motivate us and enable us to know how
well we are doing. When we don't know what they are, our energies are spent trying to determine whether we're setting the world
on fire or on our way out the door.

Standards of excellence encourage us to push beyond our own
self-imposed limits. Without them, we play it safe and never discover our true potential. We are unable to experience the joy of
doing extraordinary work.

Do You Know the Standards? and Are You Encouraged to Achieve Excellence?

	Yes	No
1. Has your manager ever told you what the standards are for your job?	❑	❑
2. Are the standards high, yet realistic?	❑	❑
3. Do you know what is expected of you most of the time?	❑	❑
4. Does your manager review with you the standards of the company, the department/ team, and the job on a fairly regular basis?	❑	❑
5. Are you encouraged to achieve excellence?	❑	❑
6. Do you feel challenged by your job most of the time?	❑	❑
7. Does your manager invite you to give input into the setting of the standards?	❑	❑
8. If you are a member of a self-directed work team, has the team clearly defined the standards for itself and individual team members?	❑	❑

If you answered "no" to more than one or two questions, you
probably get called on the carpet from time to time because you are
not meeting your boss' expectations—expectations that he or she

has not clearly communicated. Or you may be bored in your job because the standards are not high enough. In either case, you need to discuss the issue of standards with your manager.

Jack Asks for Standards

Jack's boss, Andrew, has never even mentioned the word standard. That doesn't mean, however he doesn't have ideas as to how Jack should perform his job. The problem is he doesn't share them with Jack and his ideas are always changing. Just when Jack thinks he has Andrew figured out and knows what he wants, he gets chewed out for missing the mark.

Recently, for example, Andrew gave Jack the assignment of preparing the support visuals for a presentation that the two of them were to give to division heads in a few weeks. It was the first time Jack had been asked to participate in a presentation of this nature. Since Andrew was extremely busy with other projects, Jack tried to help by handling the job himself without asking questions. He contacted the slide house and printer he had used for other presentations in the past.

Jack was given no timetable for when the slides and handout materials were to be completed or at what stages of development Andrew wanted to see them. Nor did Jack receive any guidelines as to how they should look.

When he showed Andrew the finished artwork four days before the presentation, Andrew hit the ceiling. He didn't like the typeface, the graphs were much too small, the colors were all wrong, and the list went on.

Jack had to have the job completely redone according to the new specifications which, along with the overtime charges for redoing the job on a rush basis, cost the company plenty of money.

This was not the first time Jack had been burned. This time, though, he decided to do things differently. Jack asked to meet with Andrew. He explained that he would like to develop ways he could better meet Andrew's expectations. In the meeting, Jack requested specific standards in a number of areas, such as when work was due, how certain projects should be completed, and when Andrew's approval was required.

Jack also took responsibility for some of his mistakes—mistakes he could have avoided had he only asked. He explained to

Andrew that he needs standards so that he won't have to constantly badger him. The standards, Jack argued, will also give him something to strive for and an idea of how well he is doing.

The Right to Receive the Training Needed to Meet the Job Standard

If you are going to meet the standards set for you and fulfill the responsibilities of the job, you must be trained to do so. Even if you have a wealth of experience and knowledge from another company or from another position within your current company, you still need to be instructed to meet the requirements of your present job. Training is essential to our professional growth and development, as well as to our overall feeling of confidence.

Have You Been Properly Trained for the Job?

	Yes	No
1. Do you feel you know how to do the job, and are aware when you're doing it correctly?	❏	❏
2. Do you feel you were thrown into your current position with little or no prior training?	❏	❏
3. Does your boss spend time developing you on an ongoing basis, either formally or informally?	❏	❏
4. When you joined the company or organization, did you receive a proper orientation?	❏	❏
5. Does your manager or team leader constantly set new learning objectives for you?	❏	❏
6. Do you have a real interest in your job because you feel you are still learning and growing?	❏	❏
7. Does your company place a high priority on training and development?	❏	❏

If you answered "no" to more than one or two questions, you probably feel that you are in over your head, or you feel stagnant because you aren't learning and growing. You need to enlist your manager's help in getting your training needs met.

Jack Asks for Training

When Jack accepted his current position, he didn't know he was expected to be proficient in a particular Web-based database program. Andrew just naturally assumed he already had the skills. He didn't know that Jack's precious department was the last to receive the software, which is why he never had the opportunity to learn.

Since joining the department, everything has been in such a whirlwind that Jack hasn't had time to go to a training class.

Even if he did, he would still need more training on the job, and no one has the time to teach him. Everyone else is as busy as he.

Jack is also relatively new to management. Like so many new managers, he is having to learn by trial and error. He is overwhelmed by the "people" part of the job. The company doesn't put much emphasis on training. So management development isn't a requirement for any of the company's managers, whether they are seasoned managers or completely new to management.

If he wants to survive in the job, Jack knows he must learn some new skills and he must take the initiative in acquiring them. He puts some ideas on paper as to how he plans to develop his skills, and asks to meet with Andrew to review them and gain his support. When he meets with Andrew, he explains why he wants to improve his skills and why the time and money will be well spent. Because the department is so busy, Jack recommends that he take the computer course in the evening, off premises. Once he has completed the training, he asks Andrew if he would be willing to assign someone to work with him for fifteen minutes every other day so he can learn to apply the classroom training to the job.

On the subject of management training, Jack discovered that the Human Resources Department offers an elective course on Effective Supervision. Andrew agreed to let him attend and even suggested that he take a course from the American Management Association.

Jack is interested in doing more than acquiring just enough skills to get by; he wants to learn and grow continuously. So he develops a long-term training plan and presents it to Andrew for his approval.

The Right to Receive Knowledge

Trying to do your job when you don't have the necessary information is like trying to navigate a ship without a compass. You are severely limited in your ability to fulfill your responsibilities, exercise your authority, and use your skills and abilities effectively. Success is difficult to achieve, if not impossible, when you don't have the right information, because you are unable to make sound decisions.

Do You Receive the Knowledge and Information You Need to Do Your job?

	Yes	No
1. Do you receive on a timely basis the information you need to make good decisions?	❑	❑
2. Is the information you receive complete and correct?	❑	❑
3. Do people in your company willingly share information instead of hoarding it for fear they will lose their power?	❑	❑
4. Does your manager anticipate your information needs so that you don't have to hound him?	❑	❑
5. Do you receive information about the organization's goals and objectives, as well as about the department's/team's goals and objectives?	❑	❑
6. Do you receive information regarding changes in advance so that you have time to adjust and plan for them?	❑	❑
7. Is most of the information you receive necessary?	❑	❑

If you answered "no" to more than one or two questions, you probably feel powerless because you don't have the information you need to do your job. You need to be more assertive in getting your information needs met.

Jack Aggressively Seeks Information

Like many managers in his company, Jack has a real problem obtaining information. He becomes especially frustrated when customers ask questions he can't answer. The marketing department, for example, is forever introducing new promotions and running new campaigns without telling him and his staff, which often leaves them looking grossly incompetent.

Trying to get information out of other departments is usually a major undertaking. The other day, Jack needed some figures from the accounting department. Without the figures, Jack couldn't make a recommendation to Andrew about a future expenditure they were considering, a recommendation that Andrew was eagerly awaiting. Tired of working in the dark and always complaining about not having enough information, Jack decides to aggressively seek out the information he needs instead of waiting for it to come to him. For example, he meets with the marketing department and obtains a schedule of their campaigns and promotions for the year. Periodically, he calls them to see what is upcoming in the near future.

When he needs specific information by a certain date, he puts the request in writing instead of relying on a verbal request, which can be easily forgotten and cannot be tracked. Whenever he thinks he may not be able to meet a deadline because of missing information, he lets Andrew know, in writing, that meeting the deadline is contingent upon his receiving the proper information on a timely basis.

The Right to Receive Feedback

To achieve satisfaction and success in your work, you must have frequent feedback. Feedback lets you know where you stand and how well you are doing in meeting the standards and achieving your goals and objectives. Without it, you are unable to make the necessary changes and improvements.

Do You Receive Adequate Feedback?

	Yes	No
1. Does your manager counsel you on a regular basis?	❑	❑
2. Do you receive a written performance appraisal at least once a year, and does it adequately reflect your performance?	❑	❑
3. Do you usually know where you stand with your manager?	❑	❑
4. Do you receive feedback close to the time of the event or accomplishment so that it's meaningful?	❑	❑
5. Do you feel your manager is honest with you?	❑	❑
6. Do you get feedback when you have done something right, as well as when you have done something wrong?	❑	❑
7. Do you feel appreciated and important because you receive regular feedback?	❑	❑
8. If you are a member of a self-directed work team, do you regularly receive feedback from other team members?	❑	❑

If you answered "no" to more than one or two questions, you probably live with the big question, "Does my boss think I'm doing a good job or not?" If you don't feel you are getting enough feedback, you need to gently force the issue with your boss.

Jack Asks for Feedback

Jack rarely hears from Andrew except when he has done something wrong, and then it is usually just to express anger rather than give constructive criticism. Since Andrew is known for his short fuse, Jack doesn't lose much sleep when he blows up at him, which is something Andrew does occasionally with other people as well.

Andrew stays fairly aloof from the people who work with him. For the most part, he is a loner, even with his peers. So it's difficult to know where you stand with him.

He gives Jack a written performance review every year, but it doesn't tell him much. He answers most of the questions on the form in one word or a short phrase. And he has been known to give almost identical reviews to different people.

Jack would appreciate just a short conversation every now and then to let him know how he is doing. But all he usually gets is silent indifference. Sometimes Jack feels as though his boss does not even know he is there.

It is difficult for Jack to ask for feedback. In some ways, he feels that he should know how he is doing and that he shouldn't need Andrew to tell him. But he reasons to himself, "That's silly. I'm not a mind reader. If he doesn't tell me how he thinks I am doing, which may be different from what I think, how can I know?"

With the date of his annual review coming up, Jack uses it as an opportunity to ask for more feedback. He explains to Andrew that his evaluation and opinion of his performance are important to him. "Without it," he tells Andrew, "I have difficulty knowing when I'm performing well and when I need to improve." He lets Andrew know that he wants to grow in the job and give 100 percent and that his boss's feedback is important if he is to do so.

The Right to Receive Recognition

Most people have a strong need for recognition. We need to know that we count, that we make a difference. Recognition is the reward that fuels our desire to continue to do excellent work.

It is a validation of who we are and what we have to contribute. Most people find it difficult to sustain a high energy level and superior performance without some form of recognition from time to time.

Do You Receive Enough Recognition?

	Yes	No
1. Does your manager treat you like a winner?	❑	❑
2. Do you receive recognition that is appropriate to your achievements?	❑	❑
3. Do you feel your manager is sincere in the recognition he or she gives you?	❑	❑
4. Do you feel appreciated as a person?	❑	❑
5. Is the recognition you receive equal to that given to others for similar achievements?	❑	❑
6. Do you receive recognition on a timely basis?	❑	❑
7. Does the recognition you receive encourage you to work with and support the other members of your team?	❑	❑

If you answered "no" to more than one or two questions, you probably feel taken advantage of and unappreciated. If you are not receiving the promotions and salary increases you feel you deserve, you need to ask why—in a way that does not threaten your boss. With regard to verbal recognition and praise, look to yourself for validation instead of your boss.

Jack Confronts His Boss

A few months ago, Jack achieved something at work that was one of the highlights of his career. Even some of the senior vice presidents applauded him. Jack received hearty congratulations from almost everyone, except his boss. From Andrew, he received a half-hearted nod and feeble "thanks."

Jack realized this was just Andrew's way; he hardly ever gave praise to anyone. But that did not make Jack feel much better.

Jack was also angry because everyone in his department recently received exactly the same percentage increase, regardless of how they had performed. He took it as a slap in the face, especially since he had worked ten- to twelve-hour days and made some significant contributions over the past year. One of his peers in the office next to him did virtually nothing all year and received the same increase.

The next time Jack met with Andrew, he addressed the issue of his pay raise. He explained to Andrew how he felt, asking him to explain how the raises were determined.

Except when it came to pay raises and promotions, Jack stopped looking to Andrew for praise and recognition. Lowering his expectations of his boss helped to reduce his frustration and disappointment.

The Right to Be Trusted When It Is Earned

Trusting relationships between you and other people are essential to your satisfaction and success on the job. Trust diminishes the fear of not measuring up; it is also freeing. When there is a mutual trust, you are free to devote your energies to the job instead of using that energy to protect yourself.

Do You Feel Trusted?

	Yes	No
1. Do you trust your manager?	❑	❑
2. Is he consistent in his actions?	❑	❑
3. Does he display trust by giving you the freedom to do the job without hovering over you?	❑	❑
4. Do you trust the other people with whom you work?	❑	❑
5. Are you given the benefit of the doubt?	❑	❑
6. Are you able to concentrate on doing the job instead of on how things will look?	❑	❑
7. Does the person to whom you report trust and respect your decisions?	❑	❑
8. When the pressure is on, does your boss let you do your job instead of pushing you aside and doing it for you?	❑	❑
9. Do the other members of your team trust and respect your decisions?	❑	❑

If you answered "no" to more than one or two questions, you probably find yourself in a defensive mode much of the time. You need to determine the causes of the mistrust between you and your boss, and discuss the issue openly.

Jack Addresses the Issue of Trust

Jack feels he has done everything he can to earn Andrew's trust, but he has this uneasy sense that it just isn't there. Analyzing why he feels Andrew doesn't trust him, he concludes that some of it has to do with the whole company environment. In a highly political position, Andrew must be on guard at all times.

Andrew demonstrates his lack of trust in a number of ways. For one, whenever Jack is working with him on a major project with a tight deadline, he asks for a status report every few hours for fear Jack won't complete it on time. He's also quick to usurp Jack's authority and take over when the waters start to get a little rough. A few months ago, for example, one of the executive vice presidents was putting pressure on the department to give him some information. Andrew originally gave the assignment to Jack and then took it away from him as the deadline neared.

In discussing the issue with Andrew, once again Jack is honest without putting his boss on the defensive. He tells Andrew he doesn't feel he has his boss's confidence—a feeling that is affecting his ability to give his best to the job and the team. Jack gives specific examples to justify his concern. He explains that he is confused because he has received nothing but perfect reviews from Andrew in the past. He asks Andrew if his perceptions are correct and what he can do to earn more of his trust.

The Right to Have Permission to Make Mistakes

To reach your full potential and achieve success, you must be given permission to make mistakes. Without it, you are unable to take risks and explore the limits of your own capabilities. If you live in constant fear of failure, you cannot give your best effort to the job. You are unable to experience joy in your work when you are always waiting for the other shoe to drop.

Do You Have Permission to Make Mistakes?

	Yes	No
1. Do you feel you have permission to make mistakes within certain guidelines, and do you know what those guidelines are?	❑	❑
2. Does your manager view mistakes as learning experiences?	❑	❑

3. Does your boss encourage and reward risk taking? ❏ ❏
4. Does your supervisor stand behind you when you ❏ ❏
   make a mistake?
5. Are you free of the fear of making a mistake? ❏ ❏
6. Are you able to feel secure knowing your boss ❏ ❏
   would never embarrass you in front of others
   when you make a mistake?
7. Is risk taking encouraged in your company? ❏ ❏

If you answered "no" to more than one or two questions, you probably play it very safe at work and take few risks. Consequently, you are probably living up to only a fraction of your potential. You need to discuss your concerns with your boss, and ask him to give you some guidelines for what is and is not acceptable risk taking.

Jack Expresses His Feelings About the Constant Criticism

One of Jack's major gripes is that, even when he does a superb job, Andrew always finds something to criticize. He is like a police officer on the beat looking for violations. Every time Jack sees Andrew, he wonders what he has done wrong now. Jack wonders if that is one of the reasons he is so stressed out and tired much of the time—from having to be always on guard.

It is not just that Andrew calls him on his mistakes. What makes it worse is that Jack never knows when he's going to get wrung out in front of someone else. He will never forget the time Andrew embarrassed him in front of Jack's secretary. Jack had been with the department for only a few months. He was giving his secretary instructions for the day when Andrew walked into his office and lit into him.

Jack decides he can't live this way any longer. So he musters his courage and tries to communicate his concerns to Andrew. Jack tells Andrew that he thinks he could do a better job if he knew that from time to time it was okay to make a mistake. He gives Andrew examples of times when Andrew had reacted in ways that led him to believe there were severe consequences for making any kind of mistake, such as the time he embarrassed him in front of his secretary. Jack also tells him that; if he were to have standards and receive more feedback, he would probably make fewer errors.

The Right to Be Treated with Respect

Your self-esteem and self-respect are the most precious things you have. When they are injured, nothing else seems to matter. When you feel you aren't being treated with the respect you are due, it is difficult to concentrate on anything but the anger and the hurt. That feeling can sap you of the desire to do your best. When you feel respected, you naturally want to return the respect with performance.

Do You Receive the Respect You Deserve?

	Yes	No
1. Do you feel you are valued as a person?	❏	❏
2. Does your manager respect your time?	❏	❏
3. Does your supervisor honor the authority delegated to you?	❏	❏
4. Is your boss sensitive to your needs?	❏	❏
5. Is your right to privacy respected?	❏	❏
6. Do you feel you have a right to express your feelings without retaliation	❏	❏
7. Does your boss respect your personal obligations?	❏	❏
8. Do you feel listened to?	❏	❏
9. Do you feel respected by the other members of your team?	❏	❏

If you answered "no" to more than one or two questions, you probably don't feel valued as a person. You need to determine your boundaries—the kind of treatment you will and will not accept. When people cross your boundaries, you need to find polite ways of letting them know that their behavior is unacceptable.

Jack Asks for More Respect

Andrew does a lot of things that contribute to Jack's feeling like a second-class citizen. Some of those things have to do with issues already discussed, such as not having enough authority or rarely receiving any feedback. Others are of a different nature. For example, Andrew never knocks when Jack's office door is closed; he just barges in and interrupts whatever Jack is doing.

Jack makes a list of his gripes, asks himself which ones are important to him, and discusses the selected ones with Andrew. He tells Andrew that sometimes, not always, he feels discounted as a person. He cites examples and tells Andrew how he feels in ways that don't attack or embarrass him. For example, when he addresses the issue of Andrew never saying "hello" in the morning, he says, "When you don't say hello in the morning, I feel disappointed and confused. I like to know that it makes a difference to you that I am here. When you don't acknowledge my presence, I wonder if I have done something to upset you and if I have, I need to know about it so that I can correct it." By responding in this way, Jack is expressing a need instead of a judgment.

Respecting the Rights of Others

In this chapter, we have talked about your rights in the workplace and about how to defend them in ways that will serve your career objectives. If you are in a management position, the Bill of Rights on page 37 can also be a useful management tool in leading the people who work for you. The more you honor these rights for your people, the more empowered they will be to do the job. The better they perform, the better you will be able to accomplish your objectives.

One of the best ways to have our rights honored is to honor the rights of others.

We can honor the rights of our peers by being honest and direct with them, by providing them with the information and support they need from us, by giving them a word of praise when they have achieved something extraordinary, and by treating them with respect.

We can support the people we work with in a multitude of ways. What we give will be returned to us in full measure. It may not be immediate, but eventually it will be returned to us in some form.

4

Using Positive Politics to Advance Your Career

> *Reality is something you rise above.*
> —Liza Minnelli

One of the myths about working and success that many of us, particularly women, buy into is that, if we just work hard, mind our own business, and get the job done, we will be recognized and rewarded. We pride ourselves in being our own person and in refusing to play the political game. Then, when our good performance, hard work, and fine character are not acknowledged in the form of promotions, we are hurt and outraged.

Achieving success requires more than job skills; it requires people skills and a willingness to be a team player. If we wish to advance our careers and reach our potential, we must spend time building and cultivating relationships with people. We must not confuse diplomacy and the practice of good human relations with manipulative and deceitful politics.

Here's how one woman learned to advance her career by becoming a team player and applying positive politics.

> *Sharon McGuire is angry and baffled. She just found out that once again she has been passed by for a promotion, and she can't understand why.*
>
> *Her academic credentials are among the best in the company—even better than her boss's, Bob Anderson. She graduated cum laude from one of the finest women's colleges in the Northeast and earned her MBA from one of the top ten business schools in the country.*
>
> *She brings more to her job than an impressive list of degrees. She is the old-time American work ethic personified. Give her a mountain to climb and she is in her glory. She is especially good with detail and follow-through, one of the reasons she always receives excellent reviews.*
>
> *By all counts, she should at least be pushing up against the*

glass ceiling, but she has not even left the basement. Her first-line supervisor position hardly seems worth all the years of education, the ten years of dedicated service, and her patient waiting for a position that would finally make full use of her talents and abilities. Since she is married with two small children, balancing career and family has been no small feat.

Sharon is not one to play company politics. In fact, she abhors it. She prides herself in minding her own business, sticking strictly to business, and focusing her efforts on the job before her.

Sharon cannot understand why other less competent, less committed people, including other women, keep moving up the ladder while she stays hung on a rung so low she doesn't even have a private office. She is particularly enraged when she sees those who do virtually nothing getting promoted.

Why? How did she get stuck in this boring, low-level job? She has all the right stuff, but the right stuff doesn't seem to do her much good. She's put in all that work for what? Does everyone else know something that she doesn't?

Sharon's Career Empowerment Process

Defining the Problem. Sharon's problem is that she has no political savvy. She doesn't think and act strategically in terms of her career or her job. She is so opposed to the corporate game-playing that she fails to use even simple diplomacy.

Creating the Vision. Sharon envisions herself working in an environment that fully utilizes her knowledge and skills, recognizes her achievements, and allows her to be herself.

Acknowledging and Accepting the Feelings. Sharon struggles with anger and bitterness on a daily basis. She will have to deal with those feelings if she wishes to move forward in her career. She also needs to find out why she is so critical of people who don't share her values and why she's afraid to assert herself.

Making Conscious Choices. Sharon needs to make choices that will enable her to improve her relationship with her peers and superiors, and that will provide her with greater visibility within the organization.

Stop Judging and Start Accepting

Working for companies and organizations can be frustrating and demoralizing. They often do not create an environment conducive to self-expression and personal growth. That's not to say that they are incapable of meeting our needs. Some companies do an excellent job of balancing the needs of the individual with the needs of the company, but none do it perfectly.

You need to acknowledge when something is unfair. If, however, you focus too much on the injustices of the system and on the shortcomings of other people, you give away your power. You expend valuable energy on things that are beyond your control, energies that could be used more productively to advance your own cause.

> **Damning the system and other people gets you nowhere. To succeed, you must learn to accept the system for what it is and find creative ways to work within it.**

We'll use Sharon's situation to show how a person, particularly a woman, can achieve success without compromising her own beliefs, how she can employ positive politics to move her career forward.

Sharon Changes Her Attitude

A middle-aged man in Sharon's department does absolutely nothing, and yet every few years, he gets promoted. He's been around for a very long time and has an enormous circle of corporate friends, mostly men. Not only does he do nothing, but occasionally he even creates unnecessary work for Sharon and some of her peers. It's clear to Sharon that this freeloader is where he is solely on the basis of his political connections. When Sharon has to deal with him, her behavior borders on rudeness.

Another person, a woman who works a few levels above Sharon, bulldozes everyone who works under her and gets away with it. She is a master at presenting one face to her boss and another to the people under her. The woman creates havoc for virtually everyone.

These are the kinds of situations that Sharon finds so difficult to accept. The politicking, hidden agendas, and mind games drive her crazy. Sometimes, when she goes home at night, all she does is unload on her husband about what's wrong with the company and the people who work there. One day her husband asked, "If you hate it so much, why don't you quit?" At that point, she realized she was going to have to do something different. She knew enough to know that politics play a part in every company, not just where she works. She would either have to accept that fact, get sick over it, or quit. Sharon decided to work on changing her attitude.

Define Your Career Goals and Plans

Most men begin their careers with the belief that they will be working for a lifetime. Consequently, they usually set more clearly defined career goals. Through their participation in sports, they learn the importance of having a plan and strategy, a lesson they later apply to their careers. While they are doing their current job, they are constantly looking toward and planning for the future. They see their job as a stepping stone to something else; their energies are focused on achievement, reward, and moving ahead.

Women, on the other hand, often look at jobs and careers differently. While men have no choice but to work most of their lives, women have other options available to them. As girls, they are frequently taught that their job in life is to find someone to support them, to take care of them. As a result, they often tend to be less goal-oriented. While it is changing with the younger generation, for many women it still exists. Instead of aggressively going after promotions, they often wait to be discovered and "invited" to accept promotions. Many women see their jobs more as a form of self-expression and personal growth than as a means of advancement.

> **To reach their full potential in the workplace, women must set clearly defined goals early in their careers, develop strategies and plans for achieving them, make their goals known to the powers that be, and aggressively pursue their goals.**

Sharon Stops Drifting

When Sharon accepted her first job after earning her MBA, she wasn't sure how long she would work before marrying and having a family. She also wasn't sure whether she would continue working while her children were small. It turned out that she took only a three-month leave of absence with each of her children and made the decision to continue working full time.

Her indecision about how she would manage family and career, and about how much time she would invest in each, kept her from setting specific goals. Now that she knows she is going to remain in the workforce full time, her career has taken on a new meaning and importance. She's no longer content to drift and wait for things to happen.

Sharon decides to set clearly defined goals for herself. She shares her goals with her boss, Bob, and asks his advice on how best to go about pursuing them. With his input, she puts together a plan that addresses issues such as:

- *What skills does she need to develop?*
- *How can she gain more visibility within the company?*
- *How can she make her goals known to the people that count?*
- *How can she demonstrate her ability and desire to take on increasing amounts of responsibility and authority?*

Focus on the Big Picture

As mentioned earlier, many women enter the workforce without clearly defined career goals. They tend to focus more on mastering and doing the immediate job than on planning and maneuvering their next career move. If a woman is to achieve a position of power and influence, she must look at the job and career in a broader perspective.

In terms of the job itself, women tend to be more narrowly focused and more detail-oriented. Early in their careers, most women gain legitimacy and confidence by being technical experts. Their technical expertise may even land them a supervisory position, but they may still rely heavily on their technical skill and their own efforts. They earn respect by being thorough, accurate, and dependable.

While these are desirable qualities, their technical expertise and tendency to rely on themselves rather than on others to get the job done may work against them in moving to a managerial position. If they stay in the lower-level supervisory position long enough, after a while they aren't perceived as having management potential.

Sharon Broadens Her Perspective

Philosophically, Sharon and her boss Bob are miles apart when it comes to where they think their efforts should be spent and how to communicate with higher levels of management. Bob is the consummate politician, constantly looking for ways he can promote himself and his department. Sharon rarely thinks about image, almost to a fault. In the past, her sole concern has been getting the job done. Her decisions are usually made on the basis of what is best for the job and the company. She rarely takes the perceptions of others into consideration.

A few months ago, she and her boss met with the division manager to discuss plans for the coming year. When they left the meeting, Sharon received a severe reprimand. "Why did you go into all the details about the problems we are having with the new computer system? He didn't even understand what you were talking about. You should have told him we are working out a few kinks, but otherwise it's working great," he remarked.

Sharon is beginning to realize that her approach has not worked to her advantage. She needs to look at things from a broader perspective. While she doesn't wish to be the politician her boss is, she sees that she can learn some things from him. Instead of always being completely honest and direct, she decides to be more careful about what she says to whom. In addition to thinking about what's best for the job, she's going to start thinking about what's best for her and her career. Her challenge is to manage the perceptions of others, particularly their perception of her, without being dishonest or unfair to the company.

She also realizes she needs to begin thinking and talking more strategically. Instead of impressing others with her technical knowledge, she decides to start relating on a more conceptual level. She's going to start looking at her job from the standpoint of how it contributes to the company's short- and long-term goals and objectives.

You've Got to Be a Team Player

One of the advantages men have over women is that they learned as boys the importance of teamwork. They learned how to get their individual needs met by being a valuable member of the team. Through their participation in team sports, they learned a whole host of things that they apply to their careers. The lack of these lessons holds women back because they never had the opportunity to learn and apply them—things like:

- ▶ The importance of competition.
- ▶ How to win and how to lose.
- ▶ That cooperation is important—without it, everyone loses.
- ▶ If you get knocked down, you have to get up again.
- ▶ How to take criticism.
- ▶ The good feeling that comes from being a part of something larger than yourself.

To succeed in the business world, a woman must learn to accomplish her objectives through other people rather than relying solely on herself. She must learn how to be a team player as well as a team leader.

> **No matter how good you are at your job, you still have to be part of the team: working in companies and organizations is more akin to playing football than it is to playing tennis.**

Sharon Builds Consensus

Sharon, by nature, is a loner. She is also a perfectionist. When she takes on a project, she is so focused on what needs to be done that she forgets to advise and involve the people affected by the project. She often works long hours doing the work herself instead of delegating tasks to her staff. If she does it herself, she knows it will be done correctly.

She is the best at what she does but lives too much in her own narrow world. She forgets that people's egos need stroking and that tending to the relationship side of working is as important as doing the job itself

Once, for example, she asked her boss if she could enlist the services of an outside training consultant to design a program to teach interpersonal skills to her staff. Bob gave it his okay, but there was one small problem. She failed to notify the Training Department of her plans. There was a strict company rule that all formal training done within the company had to be either conducted by the Training Department or approved by them. The Training Department was furious when they got wind of what she was doing because they were designing an interpersonal skills program that they planned to present company-wide. Because the Training Director had a lot of political clout in the organization, Bob was quite distressed by the whole event and let Sharon know it.

On another occasion, she put together an elaborate proposal for streamlining the systems and procedures in her area, but was shot down by her division head. One of the reasons it never got past the drawing board was her failure to get her peers' backing for the project prior to the meeting.

Sharon is finally beginning to get the picture. If she's going to move out of her supervisory position, she's got to stop being a solo performer and join the team. One of the ways she decides to do that is to ask herself some questions before she takes any major action. Who will be affected? How important are they to what I want to achieve? How can I get their support and cooperation?

Don't Take It Personally

For as long as a woman takes everything that happens to her at work seriously and personally, she will stay in a state of anxiety and turmoil. If she is going to live and work successfully in a world fashioned largely by men, she has to learn some of their ways of coping. That's not to say she should shut off her feelings or become hard and calloused, but it does mean she has to toughen up.

This is a difficult task for women since they have a tendency to build their lives around relationships, while men build theirs around achievement. Like men, women need to learn to work with people they don't like. They cannot allow themselves the luxury of refusing to cooperate with someone who they feel has treated them unjustly, Instead of looking at the sometimes annoying behavior of others as a personal affront, they need to look at it as part of the gamesmanship that goes on in companies, as uncomfortable as that may seem.

They also need to be careful about being overly sensitive and defensive about being women. Men will detect such an attitude like radar. A woman's resistance is only met with more of the same from them.

> When women are overly sensitive and take things person-ally, they allow themselves to be manipulated and con-trolled by the actions of other people. When they stay objective, they conserve their energy and power.

Sharon Toughens Up

Sharon's naïveté frequently gets her in trouble. She has had dif-ficulty learning that not everyone is as trustworthy as she believes herself to be.

A few years ago, she was shocked to learn that one of her associates had relayed to the boss information she had told her in confidence. Thanks to her associate, the boss found out that Sharon and her husband were considering a move to the West Coast. This didn't serve her well when she was being consid-ered for promotion, which she didn't receive, but her "confi-dante" did.

More recently, she had a cost-savings idea for the company, which she knew was a winner. Before she had an opportunity to submit it to the Continuous Improvement Committee, she casually shared it at lunch with some of her peers from another department. She was dumbfounded beyond belief when the Continuous Improvement Committee informed her that some-one else had just beat her to the punch. The idea had already been submitted, with a slight variation, of course. That little breach of trust cost her a $2000 reward from the company. Needless to say, the money went into someone else's pocket.

In both instances, Sharon felt extremely angry and hurt to the point that she had great difficulty working with them at all. She took their breach of trust very personally, as though they had willfully set out to hurt her.

Sharon finds herself constantly upset by things that someone else has said or done to her at work. After anguishing over one incident after another, to the point of almost sheer exhaustion, she decides she must do something differently. She either has to quit or find a way to deal with the problems.

Sharon decides to do two things. First, she's going to do a bet-ter job of protecting herself. She realizes that part of her prob-lem is that she tells too much to the wrong people, thereby setting herself up for hurt and disappointment. Second, when people disappoint her, she's going to look at their behavior from a different perspective. She will remind herself that what people say and do usually says more about them than it relates to her. When appropriate, she decides to stand up to people and confront the issues instead of carrying around the bitterness and resentment, which only hurt her.

Build a Strong Network

Networking with other people is one of the primary ways to empower yourself. Through other people, you create new options and opportunities for yourself. No one today can afford to be without a strong network, both personal and professional.

Through networking, you are able to increase your visibility within the company and the community. It also enables you to stay informed and up-to-date on information that is critical to your success. You are able to broaden your sphere of influence and enlist the support of people who can help you advance in your career.

On another level, networking allows you to connect with other people in a meaningful way; you have a sense of belonging, of being part of the action. Through networking, you get ideas, energy, and information from other people. You expand your world.

A strong network is like a safety net. It is one of the best insurance policies you can have during uncertain times. Through networking you create windows of opportunity.

Sharon Starts Networking

Sharon's job provides very little visibility within the company. Her quiet style and tendency to stick strictly to business at all times don't seem to help matters. Sharon doesn't even eat in the employee cafeteria. She usually eats a sandwich at her desk and works right through lunch. Because of her family commitments, she rarely goes to company functions or meetings of professional organizations and groups. Needless to say, her network is virtually nonexistent.

Sharon realizes that she must begin to initiate and cultivate more business relationships both inside and outside the company. If she were to decide to leave the company today, she wouldn't have the slightest idea where to begin. That's proof enough that she needs to develop a network.

She begins by cultivating relationships with some of the people in the company who are presently just acquaintances. Instead of staying secluded in her office all the time, she makes a point to visit with people every now and then. She's learning the art of "shooting the breeze," an activity that until now has been totally foreign to her. She has even begun to entertain some of her associates in her home.

She also makes a point to attend more company functions. When she does, as painful as it is, she seeks out the people of power and influence to introduce herself.

Sharon is also cultivating relationships with people in other companies and organizations. She has joined a couple of trade associations, which, she is discovering, are excellent vehicles for meeting people and developing a network. She has even volunteered to serve in a leadership capacity for one of the organizations.

Now that she is past the fear that often goes with introducing herself to strangers—the fear of rejection—she is finding that networking can be fun and stimulating. Not only is it enjoyable, but all kinds of opportunities are beginning to present themselves.

Find a Mentor

Nothing can turn a career around faster than a good mentor. Mentors can provide you with the wisdom, knowledge, and understanding that might otherwise take years to discover on your own. They can also give you inspiration and encouragement, and help you create a vision for your career.

If the mentor believes in you, he or she can direct you in the paths that help you realize your full potential. If in a position of power and influence, the mentor can provide you with visibility and open all kinds of doors.

In seeking out a mentor, you'll want to ask yourself these questions:

▶ Do I like and respect the person?
▶ Do I feel good about myself when I am around the person?

▶ Can I learn and grow from my relationship with the person?
▶ Politically, is it appropriate and to my benefit to align myself with the person?

A mentor relationship can be one of the most significant relationships in your life. A true mentor is a catalyst for helping you discover and make full use of your personal power.

Sharon Seeks a Mentor

When Sharon looks at other women in the organization who have achieved upper-level management status, she sees that almost every one of them had a mentor. It's common knowledge within the company that each of these women's mentors played a large part in helping her advance within the organization.

Aware that successful protegé relationships don't just happen, Sharon is trying to figure a way to establish such a relationship. There is a nice president in another department, Scott Wade, with whom she deals on a fairly regular basis. Having graduated from the same business school, he frequently asks how she is doing and on a few occasions has inquired about her career aspirations.

He seems like he would be an ideal mentor. He's known within the company as being an excellent manager and a "people" person. Many of the people who have worked for him have gone on to achieve great things.

When Sharon reviews her career goals with Bob, she asks him about his thoughts on the subject. Bob has always been supportive of Sharon; so he is all for the idea.

Occasionally, Sharon and Scott Wade see one another at alumni meetings. Bob suggests that the next time she sees him at a function outside the office she casually broach the subject with him. He recommends that she plant the seed and then let Scott take it from there.

Examine Your Style

One of the great challenges facing women in business is finding a style that allows them to be themselves and that elicits cooperation and respect from men at the same time.

Women need a style that incorporates both their feminine and masculine sides. They get into trouble when one side is more developed and expressive than the other. If their style projects only the feminine side—the nurturing, compassionate, intuitive, feeling side—they are perceived as passive, weak, and incapable of "playing ball" with the men.

If, on the other side, they disown all those wonderful feminine qualities that are so desperately needed in today's workplace and project only a strong masculine side—aggressive, rational, dominating—they are regarded as hard, cold bitches.

Women and men face the same challenge: allowing the feminine and masculine to find equal expression. For women, the challenge is even more imperative and difficult since the expectation and definition of what is an appropriate style for women are determined largely by men.

> **A woman must develop a style of dress, speech, and behavior that expresses both the masculine and feminine sides of herself. The challenge is to develop a style that is acceptable to herself and to men.**

Sharon Changes Her Image

Sharon's style definitely needs work. She is attractive, is small in stature, and has an accent that sounds like she's straight out of Gone with the Wind, *not to mention a feminine demeanor that makes the average female executive in her company look like an Amazon.*

Her style is so totally feminine that most people, particularly men, never get past her pretty face and charming accent. On top of it all, she tends to be on the quiet side. Consequently, few people are aware of her intelligence and exceptional analytical abilities.

As Sharon sets her new career goals and objectives, one of the things she decides to do is to talk with an image consultant. When she looked at other women in the organization who had "made it," she saw a definite difference in style. She is going to have to make some changes.

Without turning her into someone she isn't, the image consultant brings out some amazing changes in Sharon. Most of them are subtle, but the cumulative effect is impressive. The first thing the consultant does is attack her wardrobe. Using what she already has and adding a few accessories, the consultant showed her how to dress distinctively without drawing so much attention to her appearance that people don't hear what she says. Sharon also learns how to stand, sit, walk, and move in ways that command authority and respect. They work on lowering her voice and incorporating speech patterns that enable her to communicate more effectively. Most important, the consultant and Sharon work on her self-image so that she can see herself as powerful and confident.

In addition to working with an image consultant, Sharon also takes classes in assertiveness training for women. Her efforts are beginning to pay off, people are beginning to respond to her differently.

Joining with Others

Women, like many disempowered groups, sometimes forget the importance of supporting one another. They view one another as competitors instead of allies. If they achieve power and success in the corporate world, their attitude is sometimes, "I had to scratch my way to the top; let other women do the same." Or, if they are on the climb and frustrated with their progress, they sometimes direct their anger at other women who have made it: "She made it because she sold out. She's just like the men."

When women reject and hold other women in contempt, they are often rejecting the feminine side of themselves. Instead, their attitude should be that one woman's victory is a victory for all women. When one woman helps to empower other women, they are empowering themselves. Regardless of where they are on the road, they need to see one another as fellow sojourners on a difficult path. Even if they don't meet one another's expectations at times, they need to support one another.

> **Who better can understand and empathize with a woman's struggles and the pressures on her while trying to succeed in a man's world than another woman?**

Sharon Looks to Other Women

Sharon doesn't like some of the women in her organization who are in positions of real authority. The woman who heads her division, Sandra Martin, for example, is cold, detached, overly aggressive, and intimidating.

Other women in the organization share her opinion of Sandra. They respect her for her achievements and the tough position she holds, but tear her apart every time her name comes up in conversation.

Since Sharon is part of Sandra's division, they occasionally have dealings with each other. When they do, Sharon makes a point to say as little as possible and never tries to make conversation beyond the subject at hand. Whenever she can, she avoids dealing with Sandra at all.

During a recent meeting, when Sandra had to deliver bad news about downsizing—who would be going and who would be staying—Sharon saw a more human side of her. Sharon decided that perhaps it would be worth her while to try to develop a relationship with Sandra.

Every now and then Sharon sends Sandra an article that she thinks would interest her. When she sees her on the elevator, she strikes up a friendly conversation about something other than work. If Sandra is spearheading a large division-wide project, Sharon volunteers to pitch in and work after hours. And, when other women start to criticize Sandra, Sharon refuses to participate.

As a result of their new relationship, Sharon was in a position recently to ask a favor of Sandra. She asked her if she would be willing to write a letter of recommendation to a women's group she was hoping to join. Sandra appeared to be quite pleased that Sharon had asked her for help.

5 Getting a Life When Your Job Is Everything

If I am not for myself, who will be?
—The Talmud

Some of us are so achievement-oriented and driven toward success that our total focus is work. Our every waking moment is spent either working or thinking about work. We have little time for ourselves and other people. Our lives are like a runaway treadmill that never stops.

Impressive titles, power, and money mean little when we have no life outside work. The highs we receive from our successes may sustain us for a while, but if we neglect our basic human needs for too long, eventually our compulsive working takes its toll. Here's how Judith Gordon created a healthier, more balanced life for herself after years of self-neglect.

Judith Gordon isn't sure what's wrong. All she knows is that her life seems to have stopped working. She is exhausted all the time. Work doesn't bring her the satisfaction and fulfillment it once did. She is plagued by feelings of emptiness; nothing seems to have much meaning.

What makes matters worse is that the world looks at her with envy, as though she has everything. At thirty-five, she is one of the top female executives in her field. She travels to exciting places, wears designer clothes, and lives in a house befitting the rich and famous.

She is beginning to wonder if it is all worth it. What good is travelling to exciting places when she rarely has time to enjoy them because she is either stuck in a meeting or dashing to the airport to meet her plane? When she goes home exhausted almost every evening around 9:30 or 10:00, she wonders why she lives in such an expensive home when all she does is sleep there. And who cares about the designer clothes that do nothing for her social life because she is too busy to have time for one?

It's not just the gruelling pace she keeps. She also has some problems with the way management treats her. Although her company is extremely aggressive and highly successful, management is not very concerned about their people. While they pay Judith well, they show little consideration for her beyond what she can contribute to the company. They keep loading her down with more and more responsibilities and work. They know she does the work of three people but have done little to help ease the strain.

At this point, Judith is so tired and confused she doesn't know what to do. Maybe she needs to find another job. Or perhaps she just needs a long vacation. She knows she has to do something fast because even her health is beginning to fail. She just got back the results of an upper GI series, which showed that she has an ulcer. It is time to make a change.

Judith's Career Empowerment Process

Defining the Problem. Judith's problem is that she doesn't know how to care for herself, both on and off the job. She excels at her profession, but has little or no skills for living.

Creating the Vision. Judith envisions a more balanced, fulfilled life for herself. She wants a career that enables her to achieve and that allows her to develop some of the other areas of her life. Most of all she wants to develop healthy relationships with people outside work.

Acknowledging and Accepting the Feelings. Judith must deal with the anger and sadness she feels about all that she has sacrificed in her life to achieve career success. She must also come to terms with why she feels she must always be achieving and doing. What are the feelings from which she is trying to hide?

Making Conscious Choices. Judith must make choices that contribute to her emotional, physical, and psychological well-being. She must stop working out of compulsion and choose to do other things that will add richness and fullness to her life.

High Achievers/Low Self-Esteem

Self-esteem can be defined as an inner sense of personal worth. The cultivation of it is an inside job, having little to do with external factors such as what we possess, whom we know, or the titles we hold.

When we don't feel good about ourselves, we try to hide our feelings of inadequacy and compensate for them. One way some of us try to get rid of our feelings of low self-worth is through our achievements. The more success we attain, the more worthwhile we become as persons—or so we would like to believe. The problem is that, the more we achieve, the larger the hole becomes. Our work becomes like a drug. We get some highs and a sense of well-being from our successes, but they are usually short-lived. We keep having to achieve grander and grander things to get the same high, and the highs get shorter and shorter in duration.

High-achieving compulsive workers have difficulty reaching out for help because no one knows they need it, sometimes not even themselves. And they get rewarded for their compulsive efforts, which in turn reinforces the unhealthy behavior that keeps them prisoners.

If you expect work to provide you with all your self-esteem, you will be dissatisfied no matter what you do. You will be forever at the mercy of other people. The people who dole out the raises, promotions, and commendations will become your sources of self-worth, which is a dangerous situation; your self-worth can only come from within.

Here are some of the symptoms that may indicate you are investing too much of yourself in your work:

- ▶ You feel best about yourself when you are at work or talking about work.
- ▶ Most of your waking hours are spent either at work or working at home.
- ▶ You have few or no hobbies or interests outside your career.
- ▶ You spend little time with people with whom you share a close relationship.
- ▶ When you have worked hard on a project and it is a success, you experience a euphoric high followed by a dramatic low.
- ▶ You talk mostly about work in social situations.
- ▶ When you first meet people, you make a point to tell them how successful you are.
- ▶ When plans at work don't turn out the way you would like, you are unusually demoralized and disappointed.

▶ You usually put your job before everything else.

▶ You have difficulty relaxing on vacations.

▶ You feel angry and resentful when other people interfere with your plans to work.

One reason we don't find satisfaction in our work is that our expectations about what it can provide are unrealistic. We invest virtually our entire selves in the job and expect it to give us what can only come from within.

Judith Faces Her Emptiness

Despite all Judith's outstanding achievements, she has low self-esteem, something no one would ever suspect because she always appears so poised and confident. People often remark that she has it all—beauty, brains, and personality. In fact, some people are often annoyed by her because she always appears so "perfect."

So how could Judith not feel good about herself? She has been a "star" ever since she was a child. In whatever she attempted, she was the best. In elementary school, she was the lead in the school play. In junior high, she was the state swimming champ in her division. She graduated valedictorian of her high school senior class. In college, she came very close to making the Olympic swim team. Her life has been a never-ending series of achievements.

Not only is Judith naturally good in many areas, but she also received a lot of pressure at home as a child. Both these factors contributed to her successes. She became so achievement-oriented that she had little time for socializing and developing friends. With so much pressure on her to be perfect, she was uncomfortable around people for fear she would say or do the wrong thing. Rather than have to worry about living up to others' expectations of her, she spent much of her time alone.

As an adult, Judith has repeated many of the same patterns. She gets almost all of her self-worth from her work. It is the only time she feels really good about herself and in control. At least, that is how it felt until recently.

She spends almost all her waking hours either working or thinking about work. Her leisure activities are limited to reading novels and shopping for antiques, for which she usually has little time.

People know Judith has an exciting job with a major company, so that is what she usually talks about in social situations. Her job is her symbol to the world that she is "okay."

Judith is beginning to recognize that all these years she has been hiding behind her work and her achievements. As long as she kept up a good front, no one would see how alone and inferior she actually felt. Judith longs for appreciation and acceptance just for who she is. She is starved for intimacy and a real connection with other people.

Judith decides it is time to address some of her childhood problems, which are keeping her from leading a full life. It is a tough step for her because until now she has always been highly independent, self-reliant, and able to work things out on her own. But this time she realizes she needs the help of a professional.

Maintaining Your Self-Esteem

One of the difficult tasks most people face at work and in life is maintaining their sense of self-worth. The struggle to feel good about ourselves is probably the toughest battle any of us ever wage. We are indeed our own worst enemy.

Although others cannot give us self-esteem, they can influence how we feel, if we allow them. Others can enhance the positive, or they can reinforce the negative beliefs we hold about ourselves.

If you work in an organization where people are seen as a disposable resource, where there are no social goals and objectives beyond the profit objectives, you will have difficulty finding satisfaction in your work. You may be well compensated, enjoying excellent benefits and even a host of perks. But, if top management doesn't value and respect the individual, you will feel shortchanged no matter how much money you make. You won't be motivated to give your best to the job and to the company, which means everyone loses.

> **Regardless of where you work, your number-one priority should be the preservation of your self-esteem.**

When you allow others to erode your good feelings about who you are, you give away your power; your most valuable possession. Self-esteem allows you to protect yourself and survive in unhealthy situations. It also gives you the strength to make changes and to create better situations.

How Does Your Company Affect Your Self-Esteem?

If you don't feel good about yourself at work, you need to ask why. Does it have to do with your own general lack of self-esteem, that you carry with you everywhere, or does it have more to do with how your company treats you?

> **You need to be able to recognize when you are being mistreated; otherwise you may allow the place where you work to negatively affect your self-worth.**

Here are some of the behaviors characterizing companies that build self-esteem and those that break self-esteem:

Esteem-Building Companies

▶ People work as a team and support one another instead of criticizing and belittling one another.

▶ People express their true thoughts and feelings directly rather than veiling them with silence and sarcasm.

▶ All people are treated with respect and dignity, regardless of their titles or positions within the organization.

▶ People are allowed to challenge the system.

▶ Women and minority groups are given the same opportunities as others in the organization.

▶ Staff turnover is reasonably low.

▶ High-level executives make eye contact with and acknowledge lower-level employees in common areas such as elevators, hallways, and cafeterias.

▶ Perks separating management from non-management are kept to a minimum.

▶ High-level executives make themselves visible within the organization instead of staying locked up in their offices.

▶ Decision-making is shared throughout the organization.

▶ Top management lets people know about major changes in advance and gives reasons for the changes.

▶ When lower-level people attend meetings, their thoughts and opinions are valued and respected.

▶ When the company is on hard times, the people at the top make the same sacrifices they expect everyone else to make.

▶ Top managers tell the truth and are consistent in what they say and do.

Esteem-Breaking Companies

▶ Everyone is out for themselves; there's very little teamwork and camaraderie.

▶ People avoid direct confrontation at all costs.

▶ Respect for individuals is granted according to their positions in the organization.

▶ To challenge and question the system is to put one's job in jeopardy.

▶ There are very few, if any, women or minorities in upper levels of management.

▶ Staff turnover is high.

▶ High-level executives keep themselves separated from the rank and file employees as much as possible.

▶ Most decisions are made at the top.

▶ Top management gives employees as little information as possible.

▶ Employees are rarely given reasons for major changes, and changes are not communicated in advance.

▶ When the company is in hard times, the people at the top don't make the same sacrifices they expect everyone else to make.

▶ Top managers frequently contradict themselves and break promises to employees.

Our self-esteem is affected not so much by the big things that happen to us, but by the multitude of small things we experience every day. It's the summation of the small things that tell us how important and valued we are as persons.

Some of us are so accustomed to being treated in certain ways that we don't even recognize some behaviors as unfair or hurtful. If that is all we have ever known, it feels "normal" and we expect it.

Judith Protects Herself

Because Judith has so much invested in her work, maintaining whatever sense of self-esteem she derives from her job is very important.

Even though she is compensated well, commands an impressive title, and enjoys a host of perks, she doesn't always feel secure in her position and in her relationships with her superiors. She frequently internalizes what's happening around her; if she senses that something is the least bit wrong, she blames herself.

While Judith has some self-esteem problems that have nothing to do with work, her boss and the job environment don't help matters. Her boss, who is threatened by her talent, constantly throws sarcastic "digs" her way. Sometimes she is excluded from meetings, which she should attend, for no apparent reason. One of the executive vice presidents, who is chauvinistic, is always making reference to the fact that she is a woman, in a way that clearly states, "You are not one of us."

Judith realizes she is too thin-skinned and allows the behavior of others to have too much effect on her. She is beginning to take steps to protect herself so that her self-esteem is not constantly on the line. For example, when her boss throws her a barb, she jokingly throws one back. When she isn't incited to an important meeting, she finds out why. She doesn't take offense to every minor slight or comment. She realizes that much of what other people say and do has nothing to do with her.

Affirming Ourselves on the Job

One of the ways to protect your self-image is to give yourself messages about who you are and what you deserve. Here are some positive affirmations you can use to fortify yourself at work on a day-to-day basis. Read these five times a day for one month, and you are guaranteed to feel different about yourself and your situation:

▶ I am as important as anyone else in the company, regardless of my title or position.

▶ I have a right to be treated with courtesy and consideration.

▶ I am a unique individual and have something to contribute to this organization.

▶ I am in charge of my career and my life.

▶ I choose healthy attitudes and opinions. The attitudes and opinions of others are their responsibility.

▶ I am only one person and can only do one thing at a time.
▶ I have a right to have a balanced life, which includes more than just work.
▶ I have a right to say "no."
▶ My number one responsibility is my own growth and well-being. The more I take care of myself, the more I am able to give to the company and other people.
▶ I am fully capable of meeting the responsibilities of my job.
▶ I have choices and alternatives beyond my current job.
▶ I have a right to make mistakes.
▶ Today I will stand up for myself.

It takes more than positive affirmations to change your situation, but it is a good beginning. As one person said, attitudes are the parents of actions. You must first reprogram the way you think if you wish to change your life.

> **If you find yourself in an environment that does not furnish you with dignity and respect, you need to find ways to protect your self-esteem.**

Judith Reprograms Her Thinking

Judith has numerous negative tapes in her head that run on a continuous loop. She realizes that some of these tapes are as old as she is; many are not even conscious.

She is doing a number of different things to bring to consciousness some of the old feelings and beliefs that are keeping her stuck. One of the steps Judith has taken is to develop her own set of positive affirmations. She says them aloud to herself three times every morning before she goes to work. She has had them laminated on a card, which she keeps in her wallet. In the middle of the day and sometimes more often, she pulls them out and recites them to herself. Judith also recorded herself saying the affirmations on a tape recorder, which she plays at night while she is falling asleep. Here are the affirmations Judith developed for herself:

◐ *It is okay to make mistakes and be imperfect.*
◐ *I have a right to enjoy life.*

❯ *I am much more than my achievements.*
❯ *I am capable of changing.*
❯ *I can allow myself ample leisure time without feeling guilty.*
❯ *My first responsibility is to myself*
❯ *I am a worthwhile person.*

Is Your Job Getting in the Way of Your Life?

When you let your job manage you, when work has you constantly on the run and in a state of turmoil, you are in trouble. You have little or no time to enjoy the fruits of your labors because you are always laboring, even when you aren't at work. Your state has little to do with how hard you work. It is the stress that kills the body and the spirit.

> **When your livelihood threatens your health and sense of well-being, you must face up to your situation, determine what part you are playing in your own unhappiness and make choices.**

Here are some of the signs that your job is negatively affecting your health and your life:

▶ Feeling tense much of the time when you are at work.
▶ Skipping meals because you are too busy to eat.
▶ Feeling constantly under pressure to meet deadlines.
▶ Frequently cancelling social engagements because of work.
▶ Having little energy for the other relationships in your life.
▶ Thinking about work even when you are doing other things.
▶ Feeling that whatever you do at work is never quite enough.
▶ Constantly complaining that you never have enough time for yourself.
▶ Feeling guilty because you are unable to fulfill responsibilities in other areas of your life due to work demands.
▶ Difficulty sleeping at night because of work pressures.

When your job gets in the way of your living a balanced life, it's usually because you have allowed it to do so. Some of us don't know how to live a well-integrated life because we don't have the skills. Still others of us live in chaos and confusion in our professional lives as a way of avoiding other more personal issues.

Judith Stops Working Compulsively

Judith answered "yes" to just about every question in the survey. Most of the time she is a bundle of nerves, but she hides it well with a cool appearance of calm. Over the last few years she has lost a good bit of weight because she is always skipping meals. Other people, of course, are always complimenting her on how svelte she looks. The stress and not eating regular meals have been the primary causes of her newly diagnosed ulcer.

She is never without a pressing deadline. If someone else doesn't give her an urgent due date on a project, she creates one for herself.

She has stopped cancelling social engagements because she rarely has time to make them. Most of her friends, with the exception of one loyal, concerned friend, have stopped calling because they know she will be out of town or at the office. They are tired of hearing her voice on the answering machine.

Judith is obsessed with work, day and night, and yet she feels that she can never do enough. She feels trapped. When she sees how other people lead their lives—they have friends and family, enjoy leisure activities, and have other interests—she realizes that the life she is leading is neither normal nor healthy. She is going to have to make major changes.

Nurturing Ourselves on the Job

Work should never be totally stress-free. If it is, more than likely you aren't earning your keep. The stress, however, doesn't have to be at a constant fever-level pitch, so debilitating that at the end of the day you feel as though you have been through a meat grinder. Regardless of the situation, you can do things to ease the pressure on yourself.

Some of us work as though we are running a marathon; we hardly even stop to breathe or take a drink of water. We somehow have the idea that if we aren't suffering and making great personal sacrifices, we aren't doing the job.

We get burned out in our jobs, not because we work too hard, but because we don't know how to nurture ourselves as we go about our work.

Here's a laundry list of things you can do in the course of the day to ease the stress and replenish yourself:

▶ Get a massage on your lunch hour.

▶ Close the door to your office and take a cat nap.

▶ Take a walk around the block.

▶ Call a friend just to chat.

▶ Treat yourself to a new outfit on your lunch hour.

▶ Eat when you are hungry; never miss meals because of work.

▶ Decorate your office or work space so that it is a cheerful, comfortable place to be.

▶ Call dial-a-joke for a good laugh.

▶ Meditate.

▶ Go to a pet shop and watch the animals.

▶ Read something uplifting.

▶ Do something thoughtful for someone else without getting found out (it will get your mind off your own problems).

▶ Do deep breathing exercises.

▶ Close your eyes and listen to soothing music.

▶ Stop and look out a window at nature—the sun, clouds, trees, and birds.

▶ Send yourself some flowers.

These suggestions are not solutions to the problems that may be causing us stress, but they can provide us with islands of comfort and safety in the course of the day. When we take care of ourselves in small ways, we are able to deal with the "big" problems more effectively. When we nurture ourselves, we also reaffirm our self-worth.

Judith Nurtures Herself

Judith realizes she needs to make some major life changes. She is working on them, but in the meantime she needs to find some small ways to get relief from the stress on the job.

When she first read the list of ideas in the previous section, she thought it was preposterous. With all the demands on her time it was ridiculous to think she could engage in any of these frivolous activities. Maybe someone with less responsibility could, but not she. After all, if she were to take a leisurely walk around the block, who would hold down the fort?

Eventually, she began to realize that believing she was indispensable at work was merely a way of covering up her deeper feelings of inadequacy as a person. She also realized that her obsession with work was a way of trying to control what happened to her. On some level, perhaps not consciously, she believed that if she were always performing and achieving, she would not be rejected. When she realized why it was so difficult to do nice things for herself, she felt more freedom to make some changes. At first her small attempts to nurture herself on the job were awkward and uncomfortable. She wrestled with her old enemy, guilt. But then after a while she began to enjoy herself, and, to her surprise, she was also far more productive on the job.

She began by making standing appointments; this way she didn't have to wrestle with, "Should I or shouldn't I?" Every week, except when she was out of town, she left the office to get a manicure. Once a month, she splurged and got a Swedish massage. Judith also set a standing luncheon date every other week with an old girlfriend who works a few blocks from her office. She even joined a local health club. When things get really stressful at work, she takes off for the gym where she goes for a forty-five-minute swim.

Over time, Judith has developed the ability to listen to herself and her needs. When she feels hungry, angry, lonely, tired or stressed, she is able to recognize the feelings and do something about them. It has become almost a game to her. She looks for creative ways to give herself small rewards and treats during the day.

What We Need for a Balanced Life

Every living thing needs certain conditions if it is to grow and flourish. We wouldn't put an African violet under the sink in the dark and expect it to grow. Nor would we let a deer loose in a crowded city street and expect it to live for long. And yet we allow ourselves to live and work under conditions that are every bit as hazardous.

Few people would dispute the fact that humans need air, sunshine, regularly spaced nutritious meals, exercise, loving relationships, periods of quiet, recreation and play, and something to stimulate the mind in order to be healthy in mind, body, and spirit.

Yet how many of us spend most of our lives indoors? We travel in air-conditioned vehicles from air-conditioned homes to air-conditioned, fluorescent-lit concrete buildings where we spend a minimum of forty hours per week.

We down a cup of coffee in the morning before we leave home, followed by a midmorning sweet roll and more coffee. We may be in such a hurry we don't even stop to eat lunch. Some of us don't eat all day until we get home, at which time we consume a giant-sized meal and then we sleep on it. The most exercise some of us get is walking back and forth to the refrigerator.

Those of us who are workaholics spend virtually all our waking hours with people with whom we share no intimate connection. We slither into bed long after our partner is asleep or we sleep alone. We rarely get touched. We share the business news of the day with our coworkers, but we share with no one our hopes and our fears.

Many of us work so hard and take the job so seriously that, when we do have time to play, we don't know how. We are far more comfortable leading a high-powered meeting than we are frolicking around in a pile of autumn leaves or basking in the sun on the beach on a lazy summer day.

It's no wonder we have difficulty finding satisfaction in our work when we neglect our most basic human requirements. If we neglect even one of our needs, our entire person suffers.

A human being is like a delicate instrument that must be kept under the right conditions and constantly fine-tuned.

Judith Changes Her Lifestyle

It is no small wonder that Judith feels her life has stopped working. It never has worked very well, but at least she was able to get by; work gave her the periodic highs that kept her going. She moved at such a rapid pace that she rarely had time to think about what was missing in her life. And she had achieved what the world called "success."

Now the years of self-neglect are beginning to catch up with her. She can no longer run from the fact that her life is totally unbalanced—and unfulfilling. In the past, she has been able to trick herself into believing she had a great life: she meets fascinating people in her work, travels all over the world, and has an intellectually stimulating job. Yet the big hole inside her keeps getting bigger.

When she took the self-inventory, she was appalled to see how one-dimensional her life is. She thought to herself, "I may be excellent at my job, but I'm not very skilled at just plain living."

She works an average of sixty to seventy hours per week. With the exception of the friend she sees for lunch every other week, she rarely sees friends or family. On the weekends, she is just too tired to do anything. She sleeps until noon on Saturday and Sunday, and spends the rest of the time running errands and getting ready for the next week.

Since she joined the health club, she is getting more exercise; so that has been a positive change. Even in the summer, she rarely gets outside. She loves the beach but only went two times this year. That's about the extent of her outdoor activity.

One of the reasons she is so run down is her diet. She swings between feast and famine. Her breakfast usually consists of a glass of orange juice when she wakes up, followed by a cup of black coffee and a bagel at the office. Unless she has a business lunch, she usually skips it. When she goes out for lunch, she frequently overindulges. It's usually a three-hour lunch with a client—a lot of rich foods, two or three glasses of wine, and dessert. Since she usually gets home from work too late to fix a meal, she has yogurt or a frozen dinner that she cooks in the microwave. She can't remember the last time she cooked a meal in her home.

She's about ten pounds underweight. Of course, since that is how all the models in the fashion magazines look, she doesn't see it as a problem. For all the abuse and neglect, she is actually in fairly good health with the exception of the recently diagnosed ulcer.

She sleeps on average about five to six hours at night, which isn't enough for her. Judith needs a good seven to eight hours of sleep to feel her best. It is no mystery that she wakes up tired each morning.

Judith has just about broken the company record for accumulating the most vacation time. With the exception of a day here and there, she hasn't had a real vacation for more than two years. Vacations are actually a problem for Judith. She doesn't know how to relax and unwind. So she usually feels frustrated when she is supposed to be having a good time.

It is obvious she needs to make major changes beyond the small steps she is taking to nurture herself. She recognizes that changes won't be easy and that it will be a long process. She is going to be altering some ingrained patterns of behavior that will be very difficult to change. Judith's emptiness and despair, however, have become so painful she will do anything to get relief.

First, she goes to a nutritionist who designs a diet for her, which will be healthy, give her energy, and also fit her lifestyle.

She also plans leisure activities for the evenings and on the weekends. She keeps weekday activities to a minimum but makes a pact with herself to do something relaxing and social every weekend. Judith reestablishes some of her old friendships. She and one of her friends even buy season tickets to the theater.

Judith also begins to enjoy her beautiful home by having friends over for dinner. As she makes herself more available for life, her social circle is beginning to expand. Two interesting men are pursuing her, adding a whole new dimension to her life.

Judith needs a vacation and not just six or seven days. She needs one long enough to let her unwind and adjust to the leisure. An adventurer at heart and lover of the outdoors, she decides to go on a one-week raft trip down the Snake River, followed by a ten-day stay at a dude ranch in Colorado.

The most difficult change Judith has to make is tearing herself away from the office. She always has this compulsion to do one more thing before she leaves. She has written a contract with herself stating that she is to work no more than fifty hours per week. If she wishes to work more, she has to write her "healthy" self a letter giving the reasons why.

Ever so slowly, Judith's life is beginning to change for the better. It doesn't happen overnight, and at times she thinks it would be easier to slip back into her old routine. Then she remembers what the old behaviors got her—a life of isolation and despair, void of meaning and fulfillment.

Getting Approval from the Right Place

Some of us have difficulty achieving satisfaction in our work because of our insatiable need for approval and acceptance. Virtually all our actions and decisions are motivated by what others will think. Someone becomes a lawyer when she'd rather be a plumber. We stay locked in unfulfilling careers because it "looks good" to the outside world. We do just about anything to get the validation from others that assures us we are "okay." As long as you are looking for favor from others, you can't be authentic. If you can't be yourself, you can't fully express who you are in your work.

> **When you look to others for acceptance and approval, you let them write your scripts instead of writing your own.**

To be satisfied in your work and life in general, you must learn to get approval from the only person who really matters—yourself. When you can do that, you are free. You live from the inside out, confident that you know what is best for you. You know that you are enough, that you are okay just as you are, whether you fail or succeed.

Here are some suggestions for how you can look to yourself for approval instead of others:

▶ When you need an unreasonable amount of approval from another person at work, ask yourself, "Why?" Do they remind you of someone from your past?

▶ When you feel you haven't gotten the approval from others that you need, stop and take a few minutes to quiet yourself. In your mind's eye, picture your giving it to yourself.

▶ When you feel slighted, tell yourself that this is an opportunity to learn to take care of yourself. It's an opportunity to become inner-directed.

▶ Remind yourself that, when others give you approval or fail to give you approval, either action may have little to do with you.

▶ When you begin to feel inadequate, ask yourself, "Why?" Ask yourself why you are choosing to be so harsh with yourself. Would you treat your best friend this way?

▶ Change the messages you give yourself from messages like, "You're stupid, can't you do anything right" to messages like, "That's alright. Even the best of us make mistakes."

▶ Never compare your insides to someone else's outsides. Others may look as if they have it all together but chances are that they too are struggling with their own feelings of inadequacy.

▶ Give yourself permission to be human. Examine the standards you have set for yourself. See how realistic they are.

Getting to the place of self-acceptance can sometimes be a long, arduous journey, depending on the messages you received about yourself as you grew up. But it can be done. When you learn to accept who you are and trust yourself, life takes on new colors. As Goethe said, "As soon as you trust yourself, you will know how to live."

Judith Validates Herself

One of the reasons Judith is in her predicament is her overpowering need for approval. Judith has spent almost her entire life trying to please other people—at her own expense. To some it looked like an admirable quality, but Judith knows differently. Her people-pleasing comes from a place of fear—fear that she will be rejected.

Now she is angry, tired of trying to accommodate her boss and everyone else. Besides, it doesn't work. Even when others praise her, the empty, insecure feeling comes back soon afterward.

Judith decides to start looking to herself for approval. It is such a strong need she knows it is going to take more than a few psychological tricks. But she's determined to learn how to look to herself to get needs met that in the past she has expected others to meet.

6

Knowing When It's Time to Move On

> The people who get on in this world are the people who get up and look for the circumstances they want, and, if they can't find them, make them.
>
> —George Bernard Shaw

One of the problems some of us face in our careers is not knowing when it is time to move on. Some of us jump from job to job, believing that, with each move, things will get better. Instead of facing problems and working through them, we move on to a new situation. More than likely, we keep finding ourselves confronted with the same problems.

Still others, probably the majority of us, stay in unsatisfying work situations far longer than we should. The situation stays virtually the same, year to year, but we do little or nothing to get out.

We first need to do everything within our power to create for ourselves a satisfying work experience, right where we are. Once we are convinced that we have given it our best and things still haven't changed to our satisfaction, we need to consider our alternatives and take action. Here's how one person went through the process of determining whether or not he should move on and, if so, what he should do next.

> Frank Cranston has tried everything he can at work and still, as the song goes, "can't get no satisfaction." Actually, it's not the work but all the craziness surrounding it.
>
> Frank can't seem to get along with his ogre of a boss; they keep having one confrontation after another. He's beginning to think they have a major personality conflict that can never be resolved. Frank has tried using tact. He's tried duking it out with her verbally. He has tried making her look good. He has tried giving the job 150 percent. He even tried "the silent treatment"—showing up physically but not in spirit.
>
> Nothing Frank says or does seems to make a difference.

Absolutely nothing. He has been living in this work situation for three years, and his patience is spent and his nerves are shredded. One more mouthful of Maalox and Frank thinks he will croak. He is beginning to believe the bumper sticker on his friend's car: A BAD DAY OF FISHING IS BETTER THAN A GOOD DAY AT THE OFFICE.

Frank is not a quitter, which is one reason he has hung in at the job. He likes the work itself and the other people with whom he associates. Sometimes Frank wonders if the problem is with himself. Maybe his expectations are too high. Maybe his idea that work is supposed to be fun is just a fantasy. "Face the facts, Frank," he tells himself. "Work is a four-letter word, and so is boss."

Then he finds it hard to believe that he is supposed to feel as he does every day when he goes to the office. Is he supposed to come home every night totally exhausted, not from the work but from all the negative energy spent in dealing with his boss?

What does he do? Try a little harder? Give up his dreams? Throw away his expectations? Stay where he is and resign himself to being one of the walking dead? Should he ask for a transfer? Or should he leave the company?

Frank's Career Empowerment Process

Defining the Problem. Frank's problem is that he has difficulty recognizing when he has tried enough and when it is time to move on. He feels he has worked very hard at the relationship with his boss, but he's still not sure that leaving is the right decision. If he did, where would he go?

Creating the Vision. Frank envisions a job in which he can work effectively with his immediate supervisor and reach his full potential. The quality of his relationship with his boss is extremely important to Frank. He wants to be able to devote more of his energies to the job instead of to resolving conflicts with his boss.

Acknowledging and Accepting the Feelings. Frank must look at why he is so angered by his boss. He must also find appropriate ways to externalize those feelings so that they don't take their toll on his body. He needs to examine the possibility that perhaps he has too high expectations of other people, maybe he is too judgmental. If so, why?

Making Conscious Choices. Frank must make choices to find a work situation that provides him with a satisfying relationship with his boss and that enables him to reach his career objectives.

Looking at the Big Picture

Sometimes we become so emotionally involved in a relationship that we have difficulty looking at the situation objectively. When this happens, we must take off our emotional blinders and use the fine computer on top of our shoulders for its original purpose-rational thinking.

As you evaluate your relationship with your current manager, try to get an overall picture of how you have benefitted and how you have been deprived over time. Determine how much potential you have for growth working for the person.

If current heated issues with your manager are causing you to consider the big leap, try putting them aside as you look at the total picture. Don't make a decision until you put all your facts on paper. Here are some questions to guide you in your analysis and evaluation:

▶ How long have you worked for your current boss? How much do you have invested in the relationship?

▶ How has it changed over time? What has contributed to the change?

▶ What are the positive things your manager has done for you since you've worked for her?

▶ What kind of rapport does she have with the other people she supervises?

▶ How do you feel about your manager as a person?

▶ What kinds of things have you learned from your boss?

▶ Which characteristics of your manager do you dislike most? What are the things you like most?

▶ How do you feel about yourself when you are around your boss?

▶ How is she perceived by people higher up in the organization? What kind of future does she have with the company?

▶ How have other people who have worked for your boss progressed within the company?

> Decisions should be based on both facts and feelings. If you put too much weight on one or the other, you may make a decision that is not in your own best interest.

Frank Takes Stock

Frank admits that he sometimes lets his emotions take over and interfere with his logical thought processes. He also sees things in black and white. A person or situation is either all bad or all good; there is very little gray area. Recognizing his shortcomings in these areas, Frank decides to give the situation with his boss, Carla Hines, one last try. Right now, he is in a huff over some things she did recently—like giving him a time-consuming, "dirty" job that should have been assigned to someone else. Frank puts his current grievances on the back burner while he looks at the total picture.

Having worked for Carla for three years, Frank has a lot invested in the relationship. Though he would like to see many things changed, they have resolved problems during the time he has worked for her, but not without a lot of pain and frustration. She did, for example, respond to his request for a clearer job description, more authority, and specific standards.

In the beginning, Frank felt very fortunate to be assigned to Carla's area. She was a hot shot on a fast track; Frank saw working for her as an opportunity to learn and advance his own career. They got along superbly at first until her aggressive personality began to grate on him. When they were at meetings, for example, she constantly interrupted other people so that she could make her point. They also had differences as to how the job should be done, a tussle that was a blow to Frank's ego. Frank took her constructive criticism as an affront.

His relationship with Carla hasn't been a total wash. Because of her and the projects she has undertaken, he has received a lot of visibility. He also admits to learning most of what he knows about his field from her.

Carla knows her stuff and is highly accomplished; it is her personality and management style he can't tolerate. She is smart and she knows it. It's either her way or else. She also has *an enormous ego. She always takes center stage no matter what she does. Carla Hines has an eye on the top spot, and no one is going to get in her way.*

Frank isn't the only one who has problems with her. His peers share some of the same feelings. She is aggressive to a fault, frequently having unrealistic expectations and showing little tolerance for the weaknesses and shortcomings of other people.

He also likes certain things about Carla. He respects her intelligence and competence. She is also very honest about what she thinks and how she feels. And she always gets the job done.

Frank often feels inferior around Carla, partly because she is so accomplished and partly because of how she treats him. His own fragile ego has something to do with it as well. So he can't blame all his feelings of low self-esteem on her.

Despite all the things Frank dislikes about Carla, she is going places within the organization. Top management sees her as one of the rising young stars. Frank concludes that things could be worse. At least he is learning and has the opportunity for growth working for her. But that still doesn't change the fact that he has great difficulty getting along with her.

You Don't Have to Like the Boss

Sometimes we feel that we have to like the boss as a person if we are going to achieve satisfaction at work. When our experience doesn't match our expectations of the person, we believe something is wrong and we should make a change.

Sometimes the dissatisfaction grows from the fact that we don't know how to solve small problems, which then grow into larger problems. In our frustration, we throw up our hands and say we don't like the other person.

> **If you lack the skills needed to resolve conflict, you may leave a relationship that actually has a lot of potential.**

Some of your problems can be resolved by changing your expectations. For example, if you are constantly annoyed by the fact that the person you report to has no sense of humor and is always very formal in her demeanor, perhaps you simply need to accept her for her shortcomings. If you change your expectation and attitude toward her, her personality may be less of an irritant to you.

On the other hand, you may work for someone you like and respect as a person, but you aren't learning and growing in the job. What you get from the relationship personally—things like acceptance and respect—may overshadow the fact that you aren't getting your career needs met. Your relationship may feel very safe. Most of us will make great sacrifices to maintain our sense of security.

The real questions are, "Are you able to reach your potential in the job?" and "Are you able to maintain a sense of who you are?" In looking at your answers to these questions, you want to make sure you have sound reasons for staying or leaving your relationship with your boss—reasons beyond your personal likes and dislikes.

Frank Develops New Responses

Frank doesn't like his boss, Carla, as a person. Sometimes he's surprised by the intensity of his emotions. The smallest thing she says or does can trigger feelings of rage within him. He naturally keeps them under wraps—and drinks Maalox by the gallon.

Frank recognizes that he is not very good at resolving conflict; neither is Carla. Perhaps that's why they keep locking horns. Frank wants to learn how to relate to her differently. He decides on an experiment.

For a couple of months, Frank keeps a diary of events and corresponding feelings. Once he identifies the patterns, he develops alternate ways of thinking and reacting to situations that cause him an inordinate amount of stress. Here is what two of his diary entries look like:

Event/situation	Feeling	New thought/action
Carla discounted my ideas about new project at staff meeting	*Anger and frustration*	*Carla's inability to listen has nothing to do with me.*
		My ideas are as important as anyone else's.
		I have a right to be heard.
		I will deal with the situation by submitting my ideas in writing so that I can be sure I get my point across. I will tell her how I feel.

Event/situation	Feeling	New thought/action
When one of the executive VPs walked into Carla's office while we were meeting, she started bragging excessively	Embarrassment and anger	Carla is doing this because she is insecure, not because she thinks she is great Her bragging has nothing to do with me; so it is none of my business what she does. When she starts bragging in front of others, if it bothers me, I will think about something else.

A perfectionist himself, Frank has very high expectations of Carla as a boss. Realizing that his views may be part of the problem, Frank makes a list of what they are. To his surprise, his expectation list describes the characteristics of a saint. So he goes through the list to see which of his expectations he can lower or eliminate. It dawns on him that the fewer expectations he has and the less he dwells on what he doesn't like about Carla, the freer he will be.

Knowing When You've Given It Your Best

Insanity has been described as doing the same thing over and over and expecting different results. That's what some of us do in our jobs and relationships. We stay in unhealthy situations long after we should have moved on to greener pastures.

Sometimes we don't find fulfillment in our work because what we need is to change ourselves rather than the situation. We blame someone or something instead of confronting ourselves and taking responsibility for our own happiness. The result is that we keep repeating the same patterns.

> **You need to know that you've done everything in your own power to create satisfaction and fulfillment for yourself right where you are. Otherwise you jump from situation to situation and never find it.**

Here are some questions to help you determine if you have given your relationship with your boss every possible chance:

	Yes	No
1. Considering how hard it is for people to change, have you given your manager a reasonable amount of time?	❏	❏
2. Have you clearly defined for yourself what you need to be happy in your job?	❏	❏
3. Have you clearly defined the problems on the job and communicated them to your boss in a nonthreatening manner?	❏	❏
4. Have you given her the benefit of the doubt, or do you constantly wait for her to "screw up" again?	❏	❏
5. Have you poured all your attention and energies into doing the best job possible or have you continued to dwell on the negative?	❏	❏
6. Have you looked for creative ways to break the unspoken rules in your company so that you can feel better about yourself?	❏	❏
7. When your boss has made a positive change, however small, have you acknowledged it and expressed your appreciation?	❏	❏

If you answered "yes" to all these questions and the situation has gotten worse instead of better, don't be disappointed. And don't blame yourself. You're in the process of getting to a better place in your career, and this is just one of the stages.

Some managers simply cannot handle mature, adult-to-adult relationships with the people they supervise. You may have found that the more you acted in a mature way, the more you asserted yourself, the more threatened your boss became.

Remember, you aren't responsible for your manager's actions or feelings. The important thing is that you gave it your best shot and for that you should be proud. When you have satisfied yourself that you have done everything you could do, you are ready to go on to the next step.

Frank Determines He's Done His Best

Despite Frank's efforts to change his responses to Carla, he still can't seem to get the relationship on an even keel. They continue to be out of sync with one another. The relationship has improved marginally, but not enough to satisfy Frank.

Nevertheless, he wants to be absolutely sure he has done his part. After all, Carla has helped him advance his career and, if he chooses to leave, he will be taking some risks. As a check on himself, he answers the questions in the precious section.

He's been trying his best to improve his relationship with Carla for over a year. Regardless of whether he thinks things can change in the future, he has put as much effort into it as he is willing to give.

By analyzing his work situation, Frank has been able to define what he needs in a boss and a job. Most important, he wants to be treated with respect, something he doesn't get from Carla. Among other things, he needs harmonious working conditions; his work group always seems to be in a turmoil, rushing to meet Carla's excessive demands.

Frank can honestly say he has communicated his problems and concerns to her in as nonthreatening a way as possible. She didn't take them seriously, though, which confirmed for him that there wasn't a lot of reason to believe things would change in the future. He has tried hard to give her the benefit of the doubt, even though past experience made it very difficult. Whenever she made a positive change, he made sure he always acknowledged it.

Frank also feels good about the fact that he has given the job his absolute best over the past year and that he has maintained his integrity by breaking the unspoken rules.

He realizes he doesn't have to like Carla to work for her. His problem, however, goes beyond his dislike for her. The dynamics of their relationship are such that they are affecting his ability to do his best. He realizes that part of the problem may be caused by a lack of maturity on his part. Nevertheless, he feels he doesn't want to deal with the situation any longer. It's time to move on.

Maybe You Don't Have to Leave the Company

Most people form their opinions of the company based on the quality of their relationship with their managers. If they work for someone they don't like, they probably won't think highly of the company. In fact, employee morale in any organization is nothing more than the summation of all the one-on-one relationships between superior and subordinate.

While the person to whom you report may significantly affect the quality of your day-to-day work experience, that person may not be representative of management throughout the company. And your future with the company may not have to be limited by that one relationship.

There's danger in assuming that, if you can't work things out with your boss, you must leave the company. In some cases that may be true, but not always. Many a person has been ousted for standing up to the boss, but some have secured better positions elsewhere in the same company. In most cases these people have made themselves so valuable that management wasn't about to let them go.

Confronting the situation and asking to be transferred to another area can be tricky business. Before you ask for a transfer or decide to leave the company, evaluate your future with the company and decide if you want to stay.

Here are some questions to help you in your decision:

1. How long have you been with the company?
2. Describe your track record with the organization.
3. What kind of visibility do you currently have within the organization?
4. How much of your potential do you feel you have realized since you have been with the organization?
5. How would you describe the philosophy of top management? Do they place a priority on its human resources?
6. How would you describe the morale?
7. How is your company perceived within the industry?
8. How does the future look for your company over the next five years?
9. What kinds of opportunities for growth and advancement are available to you?
10. Overall, which is rewarded—politics or performance?
11. Are you proud of your company?

Frank Evaluates His Future

Having determined that he doesn't want to continue working for Carla, Frank's next question is, "What do I do now?"

First, he considers whether he would like to stay with his present company. Frank has skills that are transferable to other areas. There is another division in particular for which he has always wanted to work. Just recently he saw a job posting for a position requiring his skills and experience. He wonders if he could pull it off. Or would Carla try to sabotage his efforts?

Before he makes the decision to try for a transfer, he takes a good hard look at the company, his history with them, and the potential for future growth.. Frank joined the company right out of college as a management trainee fifteen years ago. During his tenure, he feels he has done fairly well. He hasn't set the world on fire, but he has risen to a position slightly above most of the peers he started out with. In his present position he has a lot of visibility, something he is reluctant to give up.

As for reaching his potential, he feels that only a small portion of it has been tapped. Even though he has done well, he knows he is capable of much. more. Top management constantly claims that people are the company's most important resource, and in many ways they lice up to what they profess to believe. They spend quite a bit of money on training and development, and the benefits offered employees are among the best.

Top management, however, doesn't have a clearly defused philosophy of management. Or, if they do, they don't communicate it downward; nor do they reinforce it on a day-to-day basis. They aren't very visible to employees, and they make very little effort to find out what employees are thinking and feeling. Top management relies on a few select people in upper-middle management to tell them what is going on in the organization. Consequently, there is quite a bit of politics. Morale is not particularly low but it could be better.

Frank's company is among the Fortune 500 and is respected for being one of the best in its industry. In social situations Frank takes pride in telling people where he works. Compared to other companies, his is on fairly solid ground despite the failing economy. The future, however, is uncertain.

Frank concludes that there are a lot of pluses to staying with his present employer, but before he makes the decision he has more questions to ask.

Weighing the Consequences

Every decision we make in life has consequences. Weighing the consequences before we take action can help us make the decisions that are right for us. Here are more questions to help you find the path that's right for you:

The Consequences of Leaving
Your Present Company

▶ What kinds of career opportunities might you forgo if you leave your present company?

▶ How will your decision to leave affect your standard of living, short term and long term? How will your retirement benefits be affected if you leave now?

▶ How much time and energy will be required to establish yourself in another position or another company? Considering the other things going on in your life, are you willing to make the commitment?

▶ If you leave your job before you have secured another one, do you have the financial means to sustain yourself? For how long?

▶ Are you willing to endure the stress and strain of securing another position if you don't already have one?

Asking yourself the right questions and responding with honest answers is the secret to getting what you want. Sometimes you have to ask questions in a variety of ways before you come up with the right answers.

The best decisions come from the gut, but they are preceded by intensive fact gathering. There is a difference between acting on our feelings and acting on our gut. When we act on our feelings, we are making a decision based on our current emotional state, which can be influenced by many things and which may have little to do with the way things really are. Our feelings have a way of distorting reality and tricking us.

When we make decisions from the gut, provided we have done sufficient fact gathering, our subconscious mind takes the facts and feelings, processes them on a deep intuitive level, and, like a magnificent computer, gives us the correct answer—the answer that is consistent with who we are and what's good for us.

Frank Does More Soul Searching

Frank hasn't ruled out the possibility of staying with his present company but he wants to evaluate all the alternatives. If he decides to leave, he wants to be fully aware of the consequences.

He considers what kinds of opportunities he may be foregoing if he leaves his company now. As a former management trainee, Frank has a lot of company money invested in him; so management have an interest in seeing him do well. A few years ago a career track was developed for him with the help of the Human Resources Department. At the time, he had every reason to believe that he would one day achieve a senior management position. Today he is not sure. If his company is bought out, which is not entirely impossible, everything could change. He's also not sure how his request for a transfer may affect his career, assuming he can get the position. In short, there are no real guarantees for the future.

Frank has a wife, two small children, and a mortgage; so he doesn't have the luxury of quitting his job before he has found another. Since he's young, he is not very concerned about how his leaving now will affect his retirement benefits. He's much more concerned about his job satisfaction, long-term earning power, and potential for growth.

Whatever it takes to secure another job, whether inside the company or elsewhere, Frank is ready to do it. He's spending too much energy on his relationship with Carla, which appears to be going nowhere. He reasons that he may as well direct his energies in a way that will pay off.

The thought of leaving the only company for which he has ever worked is overwhelming to Frank, yet exciting at the same time. When he finds himself confused and frightened over what to do, he takes time to meditate. He's a strong believer that his subconscious mind knows the answer that's best for him.

How Marketable Are You?

If you decide to take the plunge, you better know how marketable you are before stepping out into the great unknown. This is especially true if your work experience has been limited to one or two companies.

Most of us have a limited capacity to evaluate our own worth. So it's important that we gather the facts that will help us determine what kinds of opportunities are out there for us and what kind of position and compensation we can command. You'll want to look carefully at this and evaluate three things: yourself, your current situation, and the job market.

Self-Evaluation

▶ What are your skills? List every skill you can think of, including those you may not be using in your current position.

▶ What are your major accomplishments? List accomplishments in your present job as well as those achieved in previous positions.

▶ How much education do you have?

▶ Over the course of your career, on average, how frequently have you been promoted? Every two years? Every four years?

▶ What kinds of awards and commendations have you received for your work over the course of your career?

▶ How fast do you learn, and how easily do you adapt to change? Cite examples.

▶ How transferable are your skills and experience? What other kinds of positions are you qualified for?

▶ Do you have a passion for the kind of work you are currently doing, or would you rather be doing something totally different?

Situation Evaluation

▶ How much money are you earning?

▶ Is your salary comparable to what similar positions in other companies are paying?

▶ What kind of competition have you been up against when you have been promoted in the past?

Job Market Evaluation.

▶ How plentiful are jobs like yours in other companies within the same industry? Outside your industry?

▶ How does the future look for your industry? Are cutbacks anticipated?

▶ Do you want to stay with the same size company, or do you prefer a smaller or larger company? Or would you rather be doing something on your own?

You may have to do quite a bit of research to answer these questions. It may seem time-consuming, frustrating, and nonproductive, but it's essential if you are going to find a satisfying career. Like any other business endeavor, the degree of your success will largely depend on the amount and the quality of your planning.

> **Most of us have a tendency to underestimate our value and marketability. We restrict our job search to positions that are just like, or very similar to, what we have done in the past.**

You may have skills and experiences that will transfer to a number of different jobs and industries. That's one reason to be thorough in your research. You can't know what you are suited for unless you know what is out there.

Three things will give you an edge when you are applying for another position: skills and experience, flexibility, and a passion for what you do...

Skills and Experience. "Can you do the job?" is the first question a prospective employer will ask. If you can't answer "yes" to this question, nothing else matters. The employer's perception of whether or not you can do the job, however, will depend to a large degree on how you package and promote yourself.

Flexibility. This is another characteristic that is high on the list of most employers today. Because of the volatility of the workplace, with all the downsizing and restructuring, employers are looking for people who can easily adapt to change.

Passion. There is great power in passion. If you love what you do, your enthusiasm and commitment will be self-evident. You will have a magnetism and energy about you that will set you apart from others.

More than 65 percent of our communication is nonverbal. Regardless of what you say, your feelings will somehow be communicated. If you absolutely detest working for someone else or if you have no interest in your line of work, your attitude and body language will reveal your true feelings to the astute observer.

Frank Considers His Options

Frank still isn't sure whether he wants to leave the company, but he is intent on finding out whether he can succeed someplace else if he really wants to.

With an MBA, Frank has the educational credentials. He also has a good track record, having been promoted on average every two years. When he's been promoted, there have always been one or two other highly qualified candidates in the running; so he hasn't been promoted for reasons other than his competency.

If he wanted to stay in the same industry, a move right now probably wouldn't be wise; jobs just aren't that plentiful. In a few other industries, jobs in his field are more plentiful, but switching industries would entail more risks.

Frank likes working for a large company. He likes the resources and the opportunities provided by a larger organization. And he likes the work he is doing; he especially enjoys managing people.

Frank concludes that he has the qualifications to secure another position elsewhere and do quite well. The problem is the job market jobs just aren't that plentiful. If he didn't have a family and mortgage to pay, he would take the risk and leave, regardless of the economy. After weighing his situation and all his alternatives, Frank decides to take the following steps:

- Ask for a transfer within his present company.
- Seek out Carla's help in achieving the transfer so that she doesn't take it personally.
- Make a list of what he learned about himself in his relationship with Carla so that he doesn't make the same mistakes again.
- Put together a long-term plan for leaving the company when the economy and job market improve.

Frank is taking an interim step toward achieving his goals. He ultimately wants to spread his wings and test his potential, but to do so he feels he must leave the company. Now, however, isn't the right time. He is willing to make the best of the current situation while laying the groundwork for the future. Even if he doesn't get the transfer, he will feel better because he has a plan and he is putting it into action.

Taking Care of Yourself When You've Lost Your Job

> Our greatest glory consists not in never falling, but in rising every time we fall.
> —*Ralph Waldo Emerson*

Losing one's job can be a devastating experience. It can also be one of the most valuable growing experiences we could ever hope for. It provides us with an opportunity to look at ourselves, determine what is important to us, and recreate our lives. How we deal with the situation determines whether it becomes life-enhancing or life-destroying.

The secret to surviving a job loss and emerging stronger than before is knowing how to nurture and take care of ourselves during the period of unemployment. Here's how one person survived the loss of her job by learning and applying some new life skills, skills that will benefit her for the rest of her life.

Cheryl Myers was stunned. It was as though she had been hit by a grenade. A million thoughts raced through her mind as she replayed the words her boss had just spoken. "Cheryl, I'm sorry to tell you this, but we won't be needing you after today. Your job has been consolidated into a position in another department." Cheryl heard very little after that. All she remembers is something about "go to Human Resources…"

Overcome by disbelief, Cheryl sat at her desk in a trance-like state, unable to move. Her worst nightmare had become a reality. She looked around at her personal items prominently displayed in her small cubicle: a picture of her two children in the heart-shaped frame made of pewter, the small cactus plant one of her coworkers had given her for her birthday, and a photograph she had taken of a beautiful nature scene of a forest with the sun's rays streaming through the trees.

Cheryl felt her whole world had been turned upside down and hurled into space. What would she do? She had very little savings and no one to depend on financially. She and her hus-band had separated about a year ago, and there were no plans for a reconciliation. He contributed very little to the support of the children and some months not at all.

To make matters worse, Cheryl was not convinced that the explanation given for her termination was the real reason. She and her boss had been having difficulty for some time now. She wonders if her termination was really the result of a cutback. Or did her boss simply want to get rid of her?

By the end of the day, Cheryl felt she had been in a time warp. She could remember going with a friend from another department to the park at lunchtime where she finally broke down in tears. After lunch she went to the Human Resources Department, where she was "processed" and given her sever-ance package. Other than that, the day seemed like a big blur.

As she walked out into the busy city street on that cold win-ter night, she felt that her world had come to an end. Life had dealt her a blow from which she felt she would never recover.

Cheryl's Career Empowerment Process

Defining the Problem. Cheryl's problem is that she lost her job and doesn't feel she has the inner or financial resources to survive.

Creating the Vision. Cheryl's vision is that she will be able to deal constructively with her current situation and use it as a growth experience. She also envisions herself in her next position doing a better job of taking responsibility and standing up for herself.

Acknowledging and Accepting the Feelings. Cheryl must first grieve the loss of her job. She must go through all the stages of grief—shock, anger, depression, guilt, and acceptance. Cheryl may also have to grieve some of the earlier losses in her life, which she has never fully healed.

Making Conscious Choices. Cheryl must make choices to nurture herself during her time of loss and transition. By taking care of her-self she will be able to take the necessary steps toward getting another job. When she obtains her next job, she will have to make choices that enable her to protect herself. She must choose to face reality instead of avoiding it until it is too late.

Don't Go It Alone

When you've lost your job, regardless of the reason, the first thing you should do is call on your support group, the people in your life who love you and accept you just as you are, the people with whom you can take off the mask. Before you even begin to think about getting another job, you need to take care of your emotional needs. Losing a job usually hurts a lot; you need other people to help you through the pain.

For some of us, asking for help when we are down is tough. Instead of reaching out, we isolate and hide. We are afraid we will appear weak if we let people know how we really feel and that we need help. Like wounded animals, we keep to ourselves and lick our wounds. Some of us may even "growl" at others when they try to assist us and make us feel better. The problem is compounded when we feel we are to blame for what happened. The longer we stay alone in our pain and discomfort, the lower we sink into despair and the longer it takes to get out.

> **You need other people in times of loss. Asking for help when you need it is not a sign of weakness; it is a sign of health.**

If you are the type who always handles things on your own and rarely asks for help, your current loss can be an opportunity for growth. It's a chance to learn new behaviors that can bring you closer to other people. If you always try to be self-sufficient, you deprive people of the opportunity of knowing you as a human being and you cheat yourself. You can't experience intimacy with others if you never show your vulnerable, hurting side. When you admit that you can't do it alone, you realize your interdependence. You experience a sense of community, of people needing other people, and of being there for one another.

> **Your pain can be a gift in disguise. It can force you out of isolation and enable you to connect with other people on a deeper level.**

Choose carefully whom you go to for help. Some people simply don't have the capacity to get out of themselves and be there for you. They may be uncomfortable watching you express strong feelings. They may have a need to "fix" you by telling you what you should do and how you should do it. Or they may tell you how you should and shouldn't feel, which is of little or no value.

> **When you have needs and strong feelings, you must choose your confidantes carefully. You need people who can listen to you without judgment and who can validate your feelings.**

Are You Able to Ask for Help?

Here are some symptoms that may indicate you have difficulty asking for help:

- ▶ Trying to handle problems all by yourself.
- ▶ Hiding your feelings from other people when you are upset, including those closest to you.
- ▶ Feeling resentful when people try to help you, especially when you haven't asked for it.
- ▶ Going to great lengths to avoid asking people for help.
- ▶ Keeping all your problems a secret.
- ▶ When you ask for help, feeling embarrassed and extremely vulnerable.
- ▶ Viewing other people who ask for help as weak and overly needy.

Cheryl Asks for Help

Cheryl has not had an easy life. Sometimes it feels like one long battle. You wouldn't know it to look at her, though; all her scars are on the inside.

She has learned quite well to depend on herself for everything—physically, emotionally, and financially.

Luckily, in the last few years Cheryl has learned to reach out to people. It has been one of the most difficult things she has ever done, and she's still learning. When her husband began to abuse her, she reached the point where she had to ask for help if she wanted to survive. She did a number of things: she contacted the local mental health clinic where she met people just like herself. She started opening up more to her friends.

*It took a lot—a tremendous amount of work on her part—
to get Cheryl out of her isolation. But now she's beginning to
feel like she's part of the human race, not so alone and hopeless. She's learning that there are alternatives to going it completely alone.*

*One of the things she has had to learn in the process is whom
to go to for help. Experience has taught her that not everyone
is capable of giving her the support she needs. Most of the time,
all she wants is someone to listen to her, sometimes to hold her,
and most of all to accept her for who she is, which some people
are unable to do. She feels very fortunate to have found a small
group of people who are able to be there for her. It has made all
the difference.*

Putting Things in Perspective

Our jobs represent security to us; they provide our lives with
structure and purpose. When they're gone, we can easily slip into
feeling as though we have lost everything. Our equilibrium is
upset, and we lose our perspective on life. It's up to us to get it
back. Even when we are not to blame for what happened to us, we
are still responsible for how we let the event affect us.

> **It's okay and necessary to feel the feelings that go with
> losing a job. At the same time, you need to look at the
> event in its proper context.**

If you feel you have lost your perspective, here are some suggestions for getting it back:

▶ Stop thinking about what you've lost and focus on what you
still have. Make a list of the things that are unchanged, for
which you are grateful.

▶ Change the way you look at the event. Consider it a challenging experience that can teach you something new.

▶ Remind yourself that obstacles and hardships are just part of
living and that your situation is temporary.

▶ Remember that others like you have struggled through hard-
ship and emerged victorious.

▶ Make a list of the things that can never be taken away from you.
Compare their importance to what you have lost or may lose.

▶ Remind yourself that the game is not over until it is over, no matter how bad things may appear. Situations can change in the twinkling of an eye.

▶ Make a list of your own inner resources. Your job is to tap into and mobilize them as you have never done before. They are your ticket out of your dilemma.

▶ Go for a long walk in the woods or a park. Notice how things are still the same there. Let the beauty of your surroundings soak in.

▶ Talk to people about the hardships they have experienced in their own lives. Ask them what brought them through the difficult times.

▶ Get your mind off yourself. Do something nice for someone less fortunate. Your problem will not disappear, but it won't have the same all-consuming importance.

You are the one who decides how much power a situation will have over you. You can choose to let it destroy you or make you stronger.

Cheryl Finds Ways to Cope

Before she takes any action, Cheryl realizes she has to get herself together; she needs to get some perspective on her situation. She's lived enough to know that how things feel and how they really are frequently aren't the same. As she recovers from the initial shock, she begins to work on adjusting her view of the big dark event.

One of the ways she does so is by talking things over with her close friends. A couple of friends in particular are excellent at listening and asking the kind of questions that help her see that all is not lost, that there is hope. These are questions that lead her to her own answers.

She gets perspective by reminding herself of the saying, "That which doesn't kill us makes us stronger." She looks at the experience to find the lessons that at this point in her life she needs to learn. Cheryl already sees the lesson in this one: she needs to be less passive and to take more responsibility for herself. Cheryl has known for a long time that there were problems with her boss. She should have confronted the situation sooner; if she had, she may have been able to resolve the problems or make plans for her departure. Instead, she chose to live in an unhealthy situation and leave her security in someone else's hands.

She tries to get the higher view by making an inventory of what she does have: her health, two beautiful children, good friends, a good mind, marketable skills, the ability to learn. By the time she finishes her list, she is still scared but she's more hopeful.

She thinks of all the hardships she has already endured in her life. Since she has survived every one of them, she can find little reason to believe she won't come through this one. Cheryl has a sense that throughout her life she has been protected. She remembers, for example, the time she was having difficulty making the house payment and out of the blue received a check in the mail from someone who had borrowed money from her years ago. She remembers, too, that when she has been at her lowest, ready to give up, someone always came along to give her what she needed to keep her going.

Nature has always been a place of solace for Cheryl. The day after she got the news, she took a two-hour hike in the snow-covered woods near her house. When she returned, somehow things didn't look so bleak. The silence and barrenness of the forest reminded her that she was simply going through a "winter season" in her life.

Cheryl has found helping others to be one of the best attitude adjusters. Many years ago she met an elderly man who has since become a dear friend and confidante. Martin is an eighty-year-old double amputee who had lost both legs from an infection that had turned into gangrene only seven years prior. He still has an incredible zest for life and a great love for people; a chat or visit with him always boosts her spirits.

Dealing with the Family

If you have a spouse and children, your job loss will affect their lives as well. While they may be a source of support for you during difficult times, they can also create added pressures.

Telling your family the news will never rank as one of your most pleasant experiences, but it doesn't have to be as devastating as you may think. Indeed, it can be an opportunity for the family to draw closer together and learn new life skills.

What you tell the family and how you tell them will set the stage for the experiences that follow. Here are some suggestions:

▶ Convene a family meeting and require everyone to be there. Tell them you have some family business to discuss. Let them know from the beginning that this is a family concern, not just yours.

▶ Be honest and truthful. If you try to hide the facts from them, particularly children, they will experience more fear and anxiety in the long run. Children sense when something is wrong. When it isn't dealt with openly, their fears become exaggerated.

▶ Be positive and hopeful. Don't paint a picture of gloom and doom. Let them know that they may have to make some changes, but that you have every reason to believe things will turn out okay.

▶ Give them some idea of what the changes may be. For example, you may have to cut back on clothing allowances; you may not take a family vacation this year or you may take a different kind of vacation; you may move to another house.

▶ Let them know what kinds of things will not change, what they can depend on. Reassure them that they will at minimum have clothes to wear, food to eat, and a house to live in. Mom and Dad will be there for them as usual. They will continue to go to the same school.

▶ Ask them to think of ways they can contribute and discuss them. Let them feel that they are part of the solution.

▶ Let them know what you will need and expect from them. It may be nothing more than understanding when they can't have something or times of quiet when you are working at home.

▶ Ask them how they feel about what you have told them. Encourage them to express their thoughts, fears, and concerns.

▶ Discuss with them what they may and may not want to tell nonfamily members about the family situation and why.

▶ Let them know you will have periodic family meetings to keep them updated and discuss their concerns.

Periodic follow-up meetings can serve a number of purposes. They can strengthen the family unit, address fears and concerns, and keep the family updated on how things are going, both in terms of your job search and how the family members are dealing with the situation.

Cheryl Talks to Her Children

Cheryl doesn't have a spouse to share the responsibility of guiding the family through crisis. So she has to do it alone. She's fairly accustomed to doing so and is actually quite good at it. From her childhood, she at least knows what not to do.

Her two children, Peter and Dawn, ages nine and fifteen respectively, are fairly well-adjusted. One of the things Cheryl prides herself on as a mother is having always been honest with them.

On the evening following her termination, after she had a day to get herself together, Cheryl says she wanted to talk with both of them in the living room. During the meeting, she lays out the facts. She doesn't sugarcoat what happened, but she doesn't put on a sad, pitiful, "What are we going to do?" face either. She expresses her concerns but assures them that just as they had survived hard times before, they would survive this one as well.

It is close to Christmas. So she tells them they probably won't get as many presents, but they will still make it a special, fun time. She had promised to get them a dog next spring; that will have to wait for a while. They probably would not be able to go to the movies as often, but they could rent videos and have their friends over. She goes through the list of the kinds of things that might change so that they won't be surprised when they happen.

Since both of the kids are good at helping out, she asks them how they think they can contribute. Peter says he can ask Mr. Barfield down the street if he can help him shovel snow. Dawn said she wouldn't mind stopping her piano lessons for a while.

When she asks them how they feel about what she told them, Dawn's first concern is whether she will have to change schools again, as she did when they moved away from their father. Cheryl remarks that she doesn't think so, but, if she does, they will somehow deal with it. Cheryl gets Dawn to talk more about what frightens her about going to another school.

Peter always felt he had to be strong since he is the man of the family now—at least that's what his father told him.

Cheryl always has to dig a little harder to find out what he is feeling. He finally confesses that he is afraid he will have to give up basketball. Cheryl knows that playing on the basketball team means everything to him. Her response is, absolutely not.

Facing Your Fears

Every kind of loss has to do with change, the mere thought of which usually stirs up a host of emotions, particularly fear. Even positive change is unsettling; we aren't sure exactly what will happen to us and how we will be affected.

The loss of a job may mean we have to make a number of alterations in our lives, which is why it can be so frightening. When we don't deal with our anxiety, it can immobilize us. We become so overwhelmed emotionally that we are unable to think rationally and use our inner resources to get us to the next place.

Some of us can't overcome our fears because we can't admit to ourselves or to anyone else that we have them. Perhaps we were taught long ago that to be afraid meant we were weak, that to be frightened is failure in itself. So we find any number of ways to deny and avoid our feelings.

> **The only way you can get past your fears is to look them straight in the eye and go through them. There are no shortcuts.**

Here are some ways you can deal with the fears you may be experiencing as a result of losing your job:

▶ Tell yourself it is okay to be afraid. Fear is a natural human emotion. It was given to us as a way of protecting ourselves. Throughout history, the people who were of great courage were not free of fear. They simply didn't let their fears stop them.

▶ Identify your fears. When we name them, they lose some of their power. Otherwise they are like evil spirits hovering over us, convincing us that disaster is on the way.

▶ Verbalize your fear to other people whom you trust. "I'm afraid to let people know I've lost my job because they might think I'm a failure." "I'm afraid my children might think I'm a poor mother or father because I can't provide for them as I have in the past."

▶ When you become debilitated by fear, reduce it to a manageable size by writing down what you are afraid of. Write yourself a positive message in response.

▶ For each fear, determine the likelihood that it will come true. It's been said that fear stands for "false events appearing real."

▶ Beside each concern, write down the action steps you plan to take to ensure that it doesn't become a reality. Fear is the absence of a plan; action is one of the best antidotes.

▶ If you are absolutely terrified over the loss of your job, ask yourself why. In some cases, the problem may have more to do with your feelings of low self-esteem than anything else. Remind yourself that you are much more than your job.

▶ Write down the opportunities that you think may be available to you as a result of your loss.

▶ Make a list of your values. Then look at your list of fears. Perhaps some of your fears will dissipate if you adjust your values.

Cheryl Faces Her Fears

For a number of years Cheryl has kept a journal. Every night before she goes to bed, she writes about the day's events, her feelings, her hopes and dreams, any new insights she's had, and, of course, her fears. One of the advantages of keeping a journal, she's found, is that it gives her perspective on her life—where she has been and how the events of her life fit together.

Reading back over her journal also helps her to see how she has overcome her fears in the past. She can see that most of them never came to pass. Even so, she still has fears today that must be dealt with. Here's what one of her journal pages looks like:

What Am I Afraid of?
❷ *I won't be able to pay the bills, will lose my house, and end up on the street.*
❷ *I won't be able to find another job.*
❷ *My children will grow up disadvantaged because I can't give them what a good parent should be able to provide.*

❯ I will fall so far behind financially that I'll have to spend my whole life working to get back to a break-even point.

❯ Other people will think I am a failure because I lost my job.

Just putting these fears down on paper makes a difference. The fear and panic that all but paralyzed her the last few days begin to recede. Her overwhelming sense of desperation is reduced to specific concerns, which can now be dealt with. Some of the fears even look ridiculous to her.

Once she has a handle on what she is afraid of she calls one of her good friends and asks if she has a few hours to spare. Cheryl talks about her fears on the list one by one with her friend, who quietly listens as she lives out in her mind the worst things that could happen. After getting rid of some of the pent-up emotion, Cheryl is ready to look at her fears realistically and put together an action plan.

She takes a look at the first fear on her list, "I'm afraid I won't be able to pay the bills, will lose my house, and end up on the street." When she thinks hard about it, she realizes that the chances of her ending up on the street are slim. She can do any number of things to earn extra money to sustain her until she finds another permanent job. She can clean houses or be a waitress; she can do word processing on a temporary basis. It will be difficult; she might have to work two or three jobs, twelve to fourteen hours a day for a while, but she can make it.

She can also take measures to prevent losing her modest home. She can get a second mortgage; she can rent her house and move into an apartment. If she has to, she can always sell it and use the proceeds to live for a while. As she goes through each fear in the same way, one thought becomes crystal clear: "I had better concentrate all my efforts on tackling the problems instead of concentrating on all the disastrous things that could happen."

Grieving the Loss

Life is a series of losses that take many forms. We may experience the loss of relationships, lifestyle, job, spouse, self-respect, health, promotion, financial well-being, ideals, dreams, and so on. Grief is the natural human response to loss. Grieving enables us to clear away the emotional wreckage and make way for new life.

When we lose our jobs, we perhaps experience more than just the loss of gainful employment. We may lose our sense of self-esteem, our financial security, our goals and dreams, and more. So being "let go" is no small event when it happens to us. Regardless of how much we rationalize and minimize our loss by telling ourselves that others have it much worse, it still hurts.

When we grieve, it affects our entire being—body, mind, spirit, and emotions. How we do our "grief work" is learned at a young age. If we've never learned to grieve in a healthy way, our losses will be all the more painful, and we will feel the effects for longer periods of time. We can, however, learn to grieve in ways that bring healing.

The natural grieving process varies in duration depending on the degree to which our self-worth was defined through the lost job. If, for example, we looked to our work to provide us with our identity, sense of purpose, and self-esteem, it may take us longer to get over the loss than it would for someone whose life isn't built around work.

The process of grieving occurs in a cycle that varies depending on the individual. The stages don't necessarily occur in sequential order; most people go in and out of the various stages and may experience more than one at a time.

Stages of Grief

Shock. Numbness, initial panic, denial, fear, and anxiety.

Anger. Hostility and mood swings.

Depression. Deep sorrow and emotional pain, helplessness, and diminished ability to function.

Guilt and Self-reproach. Blaming oneself for the loss.

Acceptance. Feeling of freedom and renewed energy.

Physical Symptoms of Grief

▶ Hollowness in stomach
▶ Tightness in chest/throat

▶ Oversensitivity to noise
▶ Shortness of breath
▶ Weakness in muscles
▶ Lack of energy
▶ Dry mouth
▶ Fatigue
▶ Decreased sex drive

Common Behaviors Associated with Grief

▶ Appetite change and sleep disturbance
▶ Absentmindedness
▶ Social withdrawal and isolation
▶ Dreaming about the past
▶ Agitation
▶ Crying

> **It is important that you recognize the physical symptoms and behavioral changes associated with grief as part of a normal process. Otherwise you may criticize yourself unjustly and inhibit your progress.**

Here are some things you can do to help your grieving process:

▶ Accept your feelings.
▶ Allow yourself to feel and express feelings, especially anger, in ways that don't hurt yourself and other people.
▶ Talk and reminisce about "what it used to be like."
▶ Visit your old place of employment.
▶ Anticipate your losses.
▶ Acknowledge each loss and what it means to you.
▶ Seek professional help, if necessary.

There is a purpose in our grieving. Contrary to what some may think, it is not to wallow in self-pity; it is to help us to accept fully the loss. Without acceptance we stay stuck in the past. If we do not allow ourselves to grieve, we may experience the physical, emotional, and behavioral symptoms longer than necessary. Unfinished grief work can cause more loss; it can affect our relationships with other people and cause us to miss out on valuable opportunities.

Cheryl Learns to Grieve

At one time, Cheryl felt that when she came upon a hard place in her life—when she lost something—the best thing to do was to get busy and pull herself up by the bootstraps. "Just keep moving" was her motto. She was always afraid that, if she let herself feel too much, she might fall apart and not be able to get up again. If she ever did talk about what she was feeling, she felt like a whiner. She never felt she had a right to burden anyone with her problems and usually ended up feeling guilty for having done so. It was easier to just "suck it up" and be a brave soldier.

That worked for her until she started having some health problems. At the young age of thirty-five she had an ulcer, high blood pressure, and severe back pains. There was nothing particularly stressful in her life at the time; she couldn't understand why she was falling apart. She was fortunate enough to have a medical doctor who treated the whole person—body, mind, and emotions—instead of just the physical. After some probing, he discovered that Cheryl had experienced an enormous amount of loss in her life, most of which she had never fully grieved.

Her doctor recommended that she seek help for the unresolved grief, which he believed was causing some of her health problems. Cheryl was skeptical; she didn't know what he meant by "grieving." She didn't have the luxury of sitting around the house crying all day if that was what he meant. Besides, the past was the past. What could she do about it now? Why dwell on the negative?

But, since she was willing to try anything to get relief, she tried it. To her surprise, it started to work. As she went back, talking about and feeling the painful experiences of her life, she began to feel the pressure lift, both physically and emotionally. She felt a strange "lightness" about her.

Cheryl can see the progress she's made by how she's able to deal with her recent job loss. She's able to accept where she is and not judge herself so harshly. She realizes that the anger, depression, and guilt—the sleepless nights, loss of appetite, and tightness in her throat—are all part of it. Instead of fighting the feelings, she gives way to them, knowing that feeling them brings healing.

When she becomes overwhelmed emotionally, she's not afraid to pick up the phone, call a friend, and say exactly what's going on inside her. If she's on the verge of tears, instead of biting her lip, she finds a quiet place alone and lets them flow. She realizes that, just as the body heals in its own time, so do the emotions. She's doing her part by just letting them "work" at their own pace.

Letting Go of Anger and Resentment

Regardless of why you lost your job, a couple of the natural responses are anger and resentment. "How dare they do this to me?" "After all my sacrifices, this is what I get!"

If you were wrongfully discharged—the boss didn't like you, or you got caught in a politically charged situation—your anger will probably be all the more intense. Or let's say your firing was the result of a company-wide layoff, but the termination was handled in a very insensitive, unprofessional manner. Perhaps they gave you no advance warning; you just showed up one day, and they told you to pack your things. While the circumstances may vary, whenever and however we lose our job, we are going to be angry.

Anger is usually a sign that you have been hurt in some way. Just like physical pain, the emotional pain of anger serves a purpose. In the same way physical pain tells you to take your hand off the hot stove, the pain of anger tells you to preserve your integrity by saying "no" to what is happening to you.

If anger is healthy, then why is the direct expression of it discouraged, particularly among women? Angry people are a threat to others. If on the other hand they are guilty, depressed, self-doubting, they stay in their place, and others can control them. They also don't have to risk disapproval. One of the ways they deny anger is by asking questions like: "Is my anger really legitimate?" "Do I have a right to be angry?" "What's the use of getting angry when there's nothing anyone can do?" To say that we shouldn't feel angry about something is like saying we shouldn't feel hungry.

> **Anger is neither right nor wrong; it just is. Most of us never learned, while growing up, that we have a right to all our feelings, including anger.**

The real question is, "What do you do with your anger?" Do you use it to spur yourself on to action and change? Or do you cling to it and let it rob you of valuable energy that you could use to help yourself?

Here are some guidelines for dealing with the anger and resentment you may be feeling over the loss of your job:

▶ First, acknowledge that you have been hurt, that you have been treated unfairly, if that is the case. Remind yourself that you are not to blame.

▶ Write a "no-send" letter to your employer, telling the company exactly how it hurt you. Just writing the letter may be enough; it may not be necessary, or in your best interest, to mail it.

▶ Allow yourself to fully feel all feelings—anger, sadness, and hurt. Find appropriate ways to express your anger.

▶ Once you have stopped blaming yourself and you have put the blame where it belongs, try to understand your employer's action. Try to separate the person or persons from their actions. Write your understanding down on paper.

▶ Ask yourself what you are gaining by holding onto your resentment. Does it benefit you?

▶ Remind yourself that you may not have been able to control what happened to you, but you can control how it affects you and how you respond to it.

▶ After you have released the feelings, express forgiveness to those who hurt you even if it's in the form of a letter you never mail.

▶ Get on with your life.

Cheryl Lets Go of Resentments

Cheryl is angry all right. She's just not sure who she's most angry at—her boss or herself.

When she thinks about how her boss, Terri Keating, treated her the last few years, she becomes furious to the point of rage. Terri did a lot of subtle, underhanded things to her; she played a lot of mind games. Sometimes, for example, she would shake her head in disapproval and frown when Cheryl was talking in a meeting. She would be overly friendly sometimes and cold as ice at other times for no apparent reason. She was constantly nitpicking Cheryl's work and making a big deal out of nothing.

Terri usually did these things when no one else was watching. Her dislike for Cheryl was their secret; she never let anyone else see her mistreat Cheryl. This way, Cheryl could never claim "harassment" because there would be no evidence. Everything would be conjecture on Cheryl's part, which would never hold up in court. Cheryl didn't buy for a moment that her termination had to do with anything other than a vindictive woman's dislike for her.

Cheryl also blames herself for what happened. She has never been able to confront people or issues very well. In failing to face up to the difficult issues in her life, she abdicates her responsibility to herself. She rationalized her unpleasant situation at work by telling herself, "If I just do my job and work hard, everything will be all right. I'll get rewarded." She is beginning to realize that life just doesn't work that way. Being a mature, fully functioning adult means facing up to the sticky, unpleasant situations and people in our lives. It's confronting them before they have a chance to get the better of us. Maybe this is what needed to happen for her to finally get the message.

Some days Cheryl literally feels "eaten up" with anger and resentment. She keeps replaying over and over in her mind what Terri did to her. And then she flips over into self-blame; she tells herself that she probably had some of it coming to her.

Cheryl is determined to get the facts straight in her mind. Was she victimized or wasn't she? How much responsibility should she take for what happened? She comes to the conclusion that, yes, she should have addressed the situation before it blew up in her face, but that doesn't change the fact that Terri in fact treated her unjustly. No one deserves that kind of emotional and psychological abuse.

Having made it clear in her mind that she wasn't totally to blame, Cheryl writes Terri a long letter, telling her exactly what she thinks of her and how she feels about what happened. As she puts her thoughts on paper, she feels a rush of all kinds of feelings—hurt, sadness, and a lot of anger. But she no longer feels guilty, which is a great relief. After writing the letter, she goes to the gym, does an hour of aerobics, followed by a half-hour of intense weightlifting. Every time she presses a *weight, she gets rid of a little of the resentment and hatred she feels toward Terri.*

When she goes home, she thinks long and hard about why Terri would treat her as she did. Terri was known throughout the company for being a hard, cold witch, although those weren't the exact words people used to describe her. Cheryl knows things about Terri's life that give her insight into her personality. She, too, had her share of tragedies, some of them in the last few years. That doesn't excuse her behavior, but it gives Cheryl a better understanding of her. She come to believe that Terri's action had very little to do with her. Cheryl was an easy place to dump some of her rage. Cheryl had a tendency to be passive, a trait that Terri absolutely abhorred; so Cheryl was a sitting duck.

Finally, Cheryl is able to write Terri a letter of forgiveness—a letter she doesn't mail. She writes the letter for herself anyway, not for Terri. She knows she is only hurting herself by holding onto her resentment.

Living with Your "I Don't Knows"

Our "I don't knows" drive us crazy and send us into panic. When we are afraid of what will happen to us, we often find ourselves projecting into the future. Instead of living in the present moment, we live in a horrible, futuristic place created by our fears and vivid imagination.

The more afraid we are, the more we try to control. The uncertainties of our lives become almost unbearable. We play over and over in our minds all the terrible things we think may happen to us. The more we try to control, the more frustrated we become when things don't turn out our way.

One reason we have such difficulty with uncertainty is that we have been taught to believe that we can and in fact should control the people, events, and circumstances of our lives. The reality is that we have very little control, if any, over anything or anyone but ourselves. We aren't nearly as powerful as we have been led to believe when it comes to people and things outside ourselves.

When we accept this fact, we are able to experience a new sense of peace and freedom. We can then spend our energies on improving ourselves and living responsibly We no longer fret and worry over what is out of our hands. We realize it is a futile endeavor.

> **It's a strange paradox. When you stop trying to manipulate and control, when you stop trying to make things happen a certain way, you usually end up getting something better than what you were originally striving for.**

When you concentrate on doing the very best with what you have and leave the outcome to God, fate, karma, destiny, or whatever you want to call it, you find that life becomes a wonderful adventure. You learn almost to enjoy the unpredictability of life. What once were roadblocks now become necessary detours to a new and better destination.

Cheryl Looks at Life Differently

Cheryl has a lot of "I don't knows" and always has. She thinks she is finally beginning to get the message that that's what life is made of—a lot of unexpected events and uncertain situations. She has been waiting for along time for smooth sailing, for something or someone she can rely on other than herself. She often fantasizes about her knight on a white horse or a white Porsche, whisking her away to a life of peace and security. After all, isn't that what she deserves, considering all that she has been through?

She is beginning to face the hard, cold reality of life: it's not going to happen. She may meet a nice man to share her life with, but there will still be uncertainty and problems. And she will still feel lonely sometimes. She also realizes that she can never turn over the responsibility for her life to anyone else, even if he is a "prince" of sorts.

The hard, cold reality, however, is taking on a new meaning for her. It has lost some of its sting. Instead of trying to find someone to make it all better, she is starting to enjoy the challenge of taking care of herself—of treating her hardships as challenges rather than guaranteed defeats. She is learning the fine art of trusting and depending on herself while reaching out for help and trusting others.

Nurturing Yourself During Difficult Times

When we go through crises, we must take extra steps to nurture and take care of ourselves. Any kind of crisis requires an enormous amount of emotional energy, which takes a physical toll as well. When our lives are disrupted and in turmoil, we usually do just the opposite. We allow the crisis to occupy all our time and attention to the point that we neglect ourselves. Some of us operate under the belief that, if we take our focus off the problem even for a minute, it is going to catch us unaware and "get us."

If we think we are to blame for what happens to us, we may punish ourselves in ways we don't even recognize. We may stop exercising, we may stop doing the little things that make us happy, or we may deny ourselves any kind of leisure activity.

> **Your entire life doesn't have to stop just because you lost your job. The more you keep the positive aspects of your life intact, the better you will weather the storm.**

Here are some suggestions for how you can nurture yourself when you have lost your job:

- Give yourself time to just feel the feelings. Don't beat yourself up on days when you have little or no motivation to move forward.
- Get physical relief from your pent-up feelings by doing rigorous exercise.
- Don't fall into the trap of thinking you must spend every waking moment looking for a new job. Allow yourself some time to do other things. You'll be more productive in your job search and more confident when you go for interviews.
- Watch your diet. If you normally react to crisis by not eating or by overeating, take steps to eat healthfully.
- Spend time with friends who can support you emotionally. Ask them to do some leisure activities with you, perhaps some you have never done before. Change your scenery.
- Get plenty of rest. Don't be hard on yourself if you feel tired much of the time, if you can't sleep, or if you are sleeping more than usual. Accept where you are.
- Do something nice for yourself every day. Take a bubble bath, read a book, take an afternoon nap.
- Before you go to bed at night, write out what you plan to do the next day.
- Talk to friends freely about how you are feeling.
- Stay away from negative people.

Cheryl Nurtures Herself

Cheryl realizes she is entering a very stressful period in her life. She can't afford to become ill; she needs to be fully functioning emotionally, psychologically, and spiritually if she wishes to make something positive out of her unemployment. She knows that, if she takes care of herself and tends to the tasks before her, the problems will take care of themselves.

Cheryl makes a list of some of her favorite things to do, the things that regenerate her in her day-to-day life. In addition to eating well and getting enough sleep and exercise, here are some of the things she plans to do to nurture herself on a daily basis:

- ❯ *Take one hour a day to meditate and pray.*
- ❯ *Write in my journal.*
- ❯ *Call or spend time with at least one friend.*
- ❯ *Play with my Persian cat.*
- ❯ *Read something inspirational.*
- ❯ *Do something nice for someone else, even if only to open a door for a stranger or drop a note to a friend.*

She also makes a list of miscellaneous activities to do periodically:

- ❯ *Go to a museum.*
- ❯ *Watch a favorite television show.*
- ❯ *Go to a park and watch children play.*
- ❯ *Take a bubble bath.*
- ❯ *Listen to music.*
- ❯ *Go for long walks.*
- ❯ *Frequent free events at the local college.*
- ❯ *Ask for hugs from friends.*
- ❯ *Sit by the fireplace.*
- ❯ *Play the piano.*

Cheryl doesn't have a lot of leisure time on her hands; her main focus needs to be on generating income and getting a new job. She knows from past experience, though, that she has to make time for other activities if she wants to function at her best. Every time she begins to worry, she resolves to do one of the activities on the list instead, even if it is just for fifteen minutes or so.

You Have to Have a Plan

When you lose your job, you have two tasks before you: the first is to survive financially and emotionally; the second is to get a new job—presumably one that is better than the previous one.

To accomplish both these tasks, you need a plan. A lot of your anxiety comes from not having a course of action. You feel lost and hopeless because you don't know what to do with yourself. When you have a plan of attack, you immediately create a new job for yourself—the job of finding permanent employment. You have a reason to get up in the morning.

As you put together your plan, here are some of the items you will want to address:

Life Assessment. How will you go about reassessing your current lifestyle, career, and values? How will those changes impact your job search?

Budget. What's your current budget? How long do you anticipate being out of work? Based on the projected time of unemployment, what kind of adjustment do you need to make to the family budget?

New Sources of Income. What kinds of things can you and other family members do to generate new sources of income? How can you market your skills and experience to get employment on a temporary basis while you look for permanent employment?

Networking. How will you go about contacting people who can direct you to suitable job opportunities? How can you expand your network of contacts?

Research. How will you go about evaluating the job market? What kinds of industries and companies are hiring people with your skills and experience?

To satisfy each of these items, develop a separate step-by-step plan. Your plan will be a road map for getting to your destination. You may find it necessary to alter your plan and go down some unexpected roads, which is fine; your plan should not be fixed or rigid. Without a plan, however, you find yourself adrift, going nowhere. Your ability to meet the challenges of being unemployed and finding suitable employment will depend directly on the quality of your planning.

8 Using Plateaus to Transform Your Life

> *Each thing is of like form from everlasting and comes around again in its cycle.*
>
> —Marcus Aurelius

At some point in our lives, often more than once, we all feel as though life seems to have stopped working for us. The things that previously brought us joy and fulfillment have faded; our soul feels dark and restless. We long for something more.

When we find ourselves in one of these places, it is usually because we are on a plateau in one or more areas of our life. If we can look at our plateaus as natural stages of the growth process, as opportunities for redefining who we are and where we are going, we will find within them seeds for new life. Here is how one person used a plateau to transform her life.

Amy Scott has taken up some new pastimes of late. When she isn't working, she fills her hours reading one romance novel after another, watching television, and indulging in her favorite vice: chocolate. Her reason? Boredom. She will do just about anything short of quitting her job, divorcing her husband, and moving to some exotic locale to escape the tedium and predictability of her life.

She looks like a woman who should be content. She lives in a beautiful, two-story colonial home. Her husband is a decent guy who owns his own business and is fairly successful. They have a nineteen-year-old daughter in college, doing well. Amy has a middle-management position with a well-known company where she is respected and has a good track record. They have a modest vacation cabin in the mountains and take a two-week vacation every year. Neither of them has any real health problems. So what's the problem? By all appearances, she lives the American Dream.

Amy's version of her life goes something like this: "I'm forty-

two years old, have lived with the same man for twenty years, on the same street in the same house for fifteen years, worked for the same company for twelve years and in the same job for five years. Every day I go through almost exactly the same routine. My husband and I have virtually the same short, boring conversation every morning and every evening. We've seen the same friends for years and do the same activities over and over with them."

Amy is starved for challenge and excitement. She would even welcome a little danger—anything to interrupt the arid predictability of her life.

Amy is particularly frustrated at work. At one time, her job provided a place where she could have an identity of her own. It was a wonderful diversion from all the responsibilities of raising a family and maintaining a home. Her career challenged her intellectually and provided endless opportunities to be creative, but not anymore.

When it comes right down to it, she is not truly pleased with any area of her life. Amy is scared. The crowsfeet around her eyes and ever-increasing cellulite on her thighs are painful reminders that she has reached "middle age." The journey is almost half over, and there is still so much to see, do, and be.

Despite her dissatisfaction with her life, in her heart of hearts Amy doesn't want to chuck it all. She has lots of reasons to be grateful. Nevertheless, she must make some changes. Otherwise, she feels she will surely die a slow death of boredom, or she will find some way to undermine what she has worked so hard to achieve.

Amy's Career Empowerment Process

Defining the Problem. Amy's problem is that she has reached a plateau in her life and career, and she doesn't know how to get off it without losing what she has. The choices and commitments she made at another time in her life no longer bring her the satisfaction and fulfillment they once did.

Creating the Vision. Amy envisions a career and life that is challenging, exciting, and fulfilling, presumably with the man to whom she is currently married. She wants to feel alive and vibrant, that she is growing emotionally, intellectually, and spiritually.

Acknowledging and Accepting the Feelings. Amy must come to terms with why she feels frustrated and bored in her life, what needs are not being met in what areas of her life. She must also look at why career achievement has been of such great importance to her over the years, why she feels such a strong need for the approval and affirmation of others.

Making Conscious Choices. Amy must make choices that will break the routine of her life and add some new, positive experiences. She must make choices that will enable her to develop in areas of her life other than career. In her career she needs to make choices that will allow her to get more satisfaction out of her job.

Plateaus—A Fact of Life

When we think of the word plateau in the context of our lives and careers, we usually think in negative terms. It almost always implies dissatisfaction, boredom, and stagnation. We don't find the present particularly fulfilling, and we don't know what the future holds. Plateaus are usually accompanied by anxiety; we have few or no outlets for our talents and energies, and we fear the unknown.

When we refer to plateaued persons, we often make judgments and attach labels such as "has-been," "past their prime," "dead wood," "out to pasture." We assume that, because a person isn't actively pursuing a specific goal or in the process of moving upward and onward, something is wrong.

Plateauing is actually a natural process that occurs in everyone's life and career. Being plateaued is not a sign of failure. It is negative only when it becomes a permanent state.

A plateau should be a transition period instead of a dead end. It can be viewed as a platform, a foundation for building on and for preparing for the next phase of our lives. It is a time for taking stock of where we are, for reexamining our values and creating new goals.

> **When you accept your plateaus as natural transitions instead of dead ends, you are better able to create new opportunities for yourself.**

Amy Realizes Her Plateau

Amy feels embarrassed. She is not sure where she expected to be when she reached this point in her life, but she didn't expect to feel this way. She thought for sure by now she would "have it together." Instead, she feels like an adolescent raring to get at life, but not having the faintest idea how to go about it.

Sometimes she thinks it's a matter of having missed the boat. Her life just didn't come together in the grand way she had anticipated. As a teenager, she had dreams of travelling the world and of being a famous newspaper journalist, neither of which came true. She never actively pursued those dreams, but somehow she believed that one day some good fortune would drop into her life and turn everything around. Now she feels foolish for having been so naïve, for having believed in fairy tales. It's her fault for not being more ambitious, for not making things happen for herself.

At other times, Amy thinks her present state is simply a matter of immaturity. She tells herself that, if she were more interesting as a person, life wouldn't be such a bore. She berates herself for her feelings. Most women would give anything to have what she has. Maybe she is just spoiled; maybe she expects too much from life. Amy has forgotten the long periods in her life when she felt fulfilled and satisfied. She has received tremendous satisfaction from being a wife and mother and building a home. Until a few years ago, she loved her job. When she looks back over her life, it has actually been pretty good; she just can't see it right now because she is blinded by emotion.

Work is probably her biggest disappointment at this point. She always thought that when she reached middle age she would be at her prime professionally; she should be reaping the rewards from her many years of experience and hard work. She never dreamed she would have reached her ceiling this soon.

One of the ways Amy copes with her frustration is by talking to her friends. She is fortunate to have an older friend, Gloria, who has been a role model of sorts for her over the years. Amy vaguely remembers her going through something similar about ten years ago. It's hard to believe though; at age fifty, she is totally immersed in life. She is always undertaking some new project or hobby, and has continued to grow professionally. And on top of it, she looks terrific, far younger than her years.

After confiding in Gloria about her disappointments and frustration, she feels relieved. She realizes her feelings are perfectly normal. She's not going over the edge as she thought; she is simply in a transition period in her life. She's able to see her feelings as positive even though they feel terrible. They are a signal that it is time for a change. It is time to enter a new growth phase in her life.

The Three Kinds of Plateaus

There are actually three types of plateaus:

1. The Job Plateau. We plateau in our job when we have mastered it completely. There is nothing more for us to learn; it offers us little or no challenge.

2. The Company Plateau. There are no more promotions to be had. Our climb up the ladder has ended. It may have little or nothing to do with our abilities and more to do with the structure of the organization.

3. The Life Plateau. This is more complex than the other two. When we have plateaued in life, we have the sense that life is passing us by. We ask ourselves, "Is that all there is?" Little or nothing excites us.

These three types of plateaus are often interrelated. If, for example, no promotions are available to us within the company, we will eventually plateau in our job. If we feel stifled and passed by at work, it can influence how we feel about the rest of our life.

Sometimes we confuse one plateau with another. We may, for example, be bored in our personal lives and blame it on our jobs. We lament, "If only I had a different job." And then, when we get a new job, it doesn't give us the lift we expected.

> If you wish to get past your plateau, you must first acknowledge that you are on one. And then you must identify which part or parts of your life you are dissatisfied with and take action.

Amy Examines Her Life

Amy keeps trying to find a foothold to work her way out of her black hole but hasn't achieved much success. First she thought she needed a hobby so she took up stained-glass making. That didn't do it. Then she thought it was her job. She hadn't been promoted for five years; work had lost its challenge. She tried doing freelance consulting work on the side and weekends, with the thought of going into her own business. She still couldn't get out of the doldrums. Amy thought perhaps she needed a long vacation—a change of scenery—so they went to the Caribbean for three weeks. The feelings, however, went with her.

Despite the encouragement from her friend Gloria, Amy is perplexed and extremely frustrated. Whenever she's had a problem in her life in the past, she has been able to solve it. But not this one. She is beginning to believe that there is no easy solution. She's going to have to tackle this one on all fronts.

Amy intuitively knows that, if she wishes to transform her life, she is going to have to turn it upside down and inside out. Her life is in need of more than a Band-Aid; it needs a total overhaul. The thought of such a major change scares her half to death but not nearly as much as the thought of living her life the way she has for the past few years.

How Do I Know I Have Plateaued?

Whether we have plateaued in our job, in the company, or in life, certain behaviors and feelings are common to each. Some of them are:

▶ Being passive and apathetic
▶ Feeling tired much of the time
▶ Finding yourself without goals and timetables
▶ Taking longer to get things done than usual
▶ Procrastinating
▶ Withdrawing from other people
▶ Flying off the handle easily
▶ Feeling as though you are drifting aimlessly in space
▶ Being upset by little things more than usual
▶ Having a sense of being left out, that life has passed you by
▶ Thinking a lot about the past and fantasizing about the future
▶ Working exceptionally hard at staying busy and complaining about the demands on you

▶ Criticizing, being sarcastic

▶ Feeling as though you are stuck in quicksand and will never get out

---

Your periods of growth and change are almost always preceded by periods of stagnation.

Amy Gets Perspective

As Amy goes through the checklist in the previous section, she answers "yes" to just about every one. She is horrified. She feels like a negative, self-pitying, broken-down old woman ready for the scrap heap. She keeps asking herself how she could let herself get to such a place? Regardless of what she knows intellectually, she can't help feeling there is something wrong with her.

And then Amy does something interesting. She decides to answer the questions as she would have answered them five years earlier. To her surprise, she only answers five of them yes. That convinces her that this is just a phase in her life. Her present feelings and behaviors are not reflective of her usual self or her entire life. And they aren't permanent.

She also thinks back to other periods in her life when she wasn't particularly satisfied. She remembers the time very early in her career when she hated her job. It was before she met her husband; nothing seemed to be going well in her life. She recalls having had some of the same thoughts and feelings she's having today.

Perhaps the feelings weren't as disturbing to her when she was younger because she didn't have as many commitments and responsibilities. Making changes was easier then. Now she has a lot of other people to consider.

Thinking back on her life, she realizes she is in, as her friend said, just another one of those painful growth periods. Growing pains aren't just for the young; they are for everyone who wants to expand their realm of experience and to live life to the fullest.

It's a Whole New World

Today people are plateauing in their careers much faster and at an earlier age due to factors beyond their control. The explosion of the workforce due to the baby boomer generation, combined with the downsizing and restructuring of American business, is creating a fiercely competitive work environment. Today there are far more candidates, particularly among the executive and professional ranks, than there are positions to be filled. That's a tough nut to swallow for a generation of people who have come from relative affluence, worked hard to educate themselves, and expect to achieve success.

For many, an early plateau is a devastating experience regardless of what they know intellectually about the changing workplace. People expect and are accustomed to receiving increasing amounts of responsibility, money, power, and status. They also expect challenge and personal growth from their work; to receive anything less is failure. Moreover, they expect their work to give them identity and self-esteem, making the plateau even more painful.

When you plateau in your company due to no fault of your own, you must face the reality of your situation and adjust your expectations accordingly. Otherwise you live in frustration trying to achieve the unattainable.

Amy Faces Reality

From the time Amy began her career some twenty years ago, she has made a steady climb, receiving promotions and pay increases about every two or three years—that is, until five years ago. Since that time, her career seems to have come to an abrupt standstill, and it doesn't look as though it's going to change any time soon.

When she looks back on her career, the promotions seemed to have come almost effortlessly. Not that she didn't work hard and earn them; she just didn't have to concern herself that much about moving up. She knew if she continued to work hard and stay on her toes, the power, position, and pay would follow.

Today it is a new ball game. Amy works for a company that has been through three major reorganizations in the last four years. Just in the past two years, there have been two major staff cutbacks. Amy can honestly say she has worked harder than ever over the last few years, but to no avail. The promotions just aren't there. The company has introduced self-directed work teams, which are slowly eliminating middle-management positions like hers. The competition is stiffer than ever. People are fighting and playing the political game harder and harder just to hold onto the jobs they have.

When she goes by the Human Resources office every now and then, she is astounded—and a bit concerned. The office is always packed with young, attractively dressed professional people filling out applications. There obviously is no shortage of qualified candidates, particularly at her level.

Sometimes she can't quite believe it. Peaking at age forty-two? Come on. By the old standards, she already should have been promoted to senior management. Amy is finally beginning to get it through her head that working harder and harder won't get her a promotion. She is going to have to adjust her expectations or leave the company.

The Myth About Plateauing

As we wrestle and struggle with the problem of too many people plateauing too soon in their careers, we must not confuse plateauing with being promoted beyond our level of ability. They are actually the opposite of each other.

The relatively small labor force of the 1950s, '60s, and '70s, combined with the rapid growth and expansion of business, resulted in people being promoted too swiftly. People moved up the ladder so fast they barely had time to master one job before they were promoted to another. The result was that many people were promoted beyond their level of competence.

Today we are seeing the opposite phenomenon. Many people are overexperienced and overqualified. They stay in jobs longer than they should, not because of incompetence but because there is no place to go.

Much of the white collar workforce is plateaued today. It's important that we not judge them by old standards. While in an earlier time a plateaued person might have been "dead wood," the product of the Peter Principle, this is no longer a safe assumption. Many plateaued people are highly competent; far too many are overly so.

> **If you wish to remain productive, you must give yourself the respect you are due. You must change your ideas and perception of career plateaus.**

Amy Understands Her Plateau

Amy isn't alone in her dilemma at work. Many of her peers are experiencing the same disappointment. Some of them are highly qualified and accomplished. It seems like such a waste—all that education, experience, and talent going unused and unrewarded.

When Amy was first coming up in the ranks, she remembers working for a man who had been in the same job for seven years. He was then about the age she is now. Amy always knew why he hadn't been promoted further—he could barely do the job he had. She liked him as a person but had little respect for him professionally. She vowed she would never become like him. She often thought of the humiliation he must have felt; everyone knew he was going nowhere. No one wanted to do the dirty job of firing him, and times were good enough that the company could easily keep him employed. He probably stayed in the same job until he retired.

Amy wonders if some people in the organization, particularly the younger people, look at her in the same way. When she was on the rise, she got a lot of attention and recognition; everyone wanted to stay in good favor with the people who were going places in the organization. But not anymore. Today she feels like one of the rank and file.

One of the problems is that management hasn't yet found any new and different ways to reward people like Amy. They are so busy just trying to keep the business afloat, they haven't been able to address the morale problems caused by the flattening and shrinking of the organization. While their efforts to create a more empowered culture and to organize the company around the team concept are well-intended, they have tried to make the transition too quickly. Managers like Amy feel threatened by their loss of power and status, while the employees feel overwhelmed by their increased responsibilities. The result has been chaos, confusion, and demoralization of the entire staff.

Whenever Amy gets the feeling that maybe she just doesn't have it anymore, she gives herself a reality check by looking at all the qualified people around her who aren't getting promoted either. She hasn't stopped growing; the organization has.

Obsessed with Promotion

For many people, getting promoted is the single most important indicator of success. It is the only way we know to "win" in the workplace.

It hasn't always been that way. There was a time, during the Depression, for example, when success meant survival. Today we look to our work to provide us with all kinds of other things such as our identity and sense of pride. Our feelings of pride depend largely on being promoted, on achieving more prestigious job titles, larger salaries, and more perks. Promotions at work carry the same importance as grades in school: they are outward symbols of what we have achieved. They tell the world we are "doing well."

When people stop being promoted, which is happening more and more, they become angry and depressed. They feel betrayed by their companies or organizations. Their employers broke the sacred "promise" that hard work would be rewarded. People feel that their companies don't appreciate and value them because they no longer reward them in the traditional way.

Learning to live without constant promotion can oblige you to learn to live as a more inner-directed being. It is an opportunity to learn to validate yourself without recognition from the outside world. When you depend on promotions for your sense of direction and purpose, you let other people establish your goals for you; your goals become implicit in the promotion. As long as your company creates your goals, you don't have to take total responsibility for yourself.

When you come to the end of your promotions, you must create new ways to gain self-esteem. You must develop new criteria for success. You must redefine what you want from your job and create goals for yourself.

Amy Acknowledges Her Competitiveness

Amy has always been highly competitive, even when a child. If she played a game, she played to win. She took her participation in sports very seriously. She had to be the best no matter what she did.

When she started her career, she became even more competitive. She had to be. She was one of only a few women in a male-dominated industry. All her peers were highly intelligent, well-educated, and totally consumed with achieving

power, status, and money—before they were thirty. Just walking into the office, one could feel the intensity. One had the
sense that everyone was rushing to get somewhere and get
there first. It was understood by all that work was a game, a
kind of race. The idea was to win, and the way you won was
by getting promoted.

Amy played the game right along with the "boys" and kept
up quite well. That's one of the reasons she only had one
child. If she wanted to compete, she couldn't be totally
engulfed by home and family obligations. One child would be
time-consuming enough.

Now that Amy is no longer getting promoted, she is beginning to feel like the race is over and she is the loser. Despite
what she knows about the condition of the industry and her
company, she can't get used to the fact that there are no more
steps to climb and no more trophies to bring home. Her whole
life has been centered around winning and achieving. The
change has been a severe blow to her ego.

Secretly, Amy has known for a long time that she has been
too competitive for her own good. She has invested too much in
winning. She feared this would happen one day and wondered
what she would do when it did. She just didn't think it would
happen this soon.

Amy decides to use the experience as an opportunity to learn
some things about herself, such as why she feels as though she
has to win in order to be "okay." And why hasn't she ever been
able to enjoy where she was because she was already thinking
about the next position?

She is determined to learn how to reward and validate herself. When she can do that, she knows she will have achieved
real freedom. She will feel good about who she is whether she
gets promoted or not.

Putting the Challenge Back in Your Job

Plateauing in the job can happen to just about anyone, sometimes as a result of being plateaued within the company. Even successful people who are experts in their fields experience job
plateauing. Although they may be working and functioning at a
high level, the repetitiousness of their jobs and the lack of challenge leave them feeling as though something is missing.

You may not be able to do anything about the fact that there are no more promotions within the organization, but you can do something about the job you have. Like anything else in life, your job experiences are what you make of them.

There are career rewards beyond promotions, some of which can be even more enriching. Within the context of your present job, you can continue to learn, grow, and take risks. Striving for these changes requires a new attitude, but it can be acquired. You can create your own challenges instead of waiting for the organization to create them for you.

As more and more people become plateaued, organizations are going to have to find new ways to stimulate and reward workers. Some are beginning to do so. In the meantime, here are some things you can do for yourself:

▶ Set new goals for yourself in the job.

▶ Look for ways you can do your job faster and more efficiently.

▶ Look for a need that is not being met in your department. See if you can create new and different responsibilities for yourself.

▶ If you are a member of a self-directed work team, try to learn as many of the tasks performed by the team as you can.

▶ Ask your boss if you can attend outside seminars in your field so that you can stay up-to-date and continue learning.

▶ Ask your boss if you can learn some other jobs in the department, provided you have yours under control.

▶ Look at the problems your company may be experiencing as opportunities for you. Look for ways that you can be part of the solution.

▶ Watch for opportunities to move within the company as a way of creating new learning experiences for yourself and increasing your marketability.

When you have plateaued in your job, it is up to you to create new situations and challenges for yourself.

Amy Creates New Opportunities

Amy is tired of hearing herself complain about her boring job. She is sick of bemoaning the fact that management doesn't appreciate her efforts and hard work anymore.

She considers going to another company but, given the state of the industry, she doesn't think things would be much better anyplace else. She decides to stay and make the best of what she has.

The first thing she does is change her attitude. Instead of looking at what she doesn't like about her job, she makes a list of all the positive aspects. Then she looks for ways she can change her present job. What can she do to enlarge and expand it, even if it means doing more work for the same amount of money?

Amy has recently been assigned to a self-directed work team. She successfully maneuvers herself into the position of team leader, providing her with a whole new set of challenges and learning experiences. She finds that leading a team is much more difficult than managing people in the traditional sense. She also looks for ways she can help the company solve some of its problems, even if the problems aren't in her area. Since she has been with the company long enough to understand more than just the workings of her own team, she is able to contribute quite a few ideas.

As a result of Amy's initiative, she eventually creates a new position for herself. It is a lateral move, but it gives her new challenges and opportunities to learn. It is a victory of sorts for Amy. She may not have gotten a promotion, but she has created her own stimulating and rewarding job. She feels like a real entrepreneur. Who knows where her new position might take her in the future?

When You've Plateaued in Life

Life plateaus are usually the most difficult because they touch virtually every area of our lives. We are tired of our work, bored with our relationships, and disenchanted with our home lives. We can't find a "cure" anywhere. Life feels like an endless stream of repetitive activities that hold no particular meaning for us. We can't seem to drum up passion in any area of our lives. Our commitments feel like a ball and chain. The worst part is that we foresee no change. If we try to look into the future, we see ourselves living the same boring existence.

We can be highly successful, even busy in our lives, and still feel plateaued. Our feelings have less to do with what we are doing than with what the activities mean to us.

> **You become plateaued when life becomes too predictable,
> when there is little or no risk and challenge.**

Most of us want and need some sense of security and predictability in our lives. A certain amount of stability in some part of our lives enables us to take risks in other areas. At the same time we need some risk and growth to keep life stimulating and interesting.

When you reach plateaus in life, you need to adjust the balance between the amount of risk and the amount of certainty in your life, between the degree of mastery and the degree of challenge.

You get past your plateaus in life by increasing your capacity to experience, to understand, to be, by exploring and expanding the dimensions of your inner self. The more you broaden yourself, the less likely—or we should say the less frequently—you will become life plateaued. When you are interested, involved, and engaged in life, there is always something new and exciting waiting for you around the corner. Life becomes less linear and more multidimensional.

Amy Creates a New Life

Amy's life is definitely predictable. She knows where she will be and when she will be there. Organization is one of Amy's strengths, so her daily routine happens like clockwork. Everything gets done, done well, and according to schedule.

Her life is also secure. She and her husband aren't wealthy, but they are very comfortable. Most of the romance has gone out of their marriage, but their relationship is still fairly stable. In short, there is very little danger in Amy's life. One day seems to fade into another with few upheavals and crises.

Outside her home and family, most of Amy's time and attention are devoted to work. She's never had many hobbies and outside interests, because she says, she has never had time. She has three primary roles in life: wife, mother, and career person. Her roles dictate how she allocates her time.

Amy has always admired other women, like her older friend Gloria, who have a lot of different interests and hobbies. Amy has been so work-oriented most of her life that, when she does try something new (which isn't very often), she feels awkward. She realizes she has limited herself by restricting her activities to her prescribed roles. When she goes outside her roles, she feels uncomfortable.

Amy realizes she may have to go through a period of intense emotional and psychological change if she is to get the fire back in her life. She is going to have to question everything—her lifestyle, her values, and what she wants to do with her life. She will have to examine the roles she plays and how she plays them. Does she want to continue to play them?

As Amy begins to change, her relationship with her husband becomes strained. He can't understand what has happened to her. She just isn't the person she used to be. She keeps coming up with all these crazy ideas about what she wants to do with the rest of her life. At Amy's suggestion, her husband agrees to see a marriage counselor with her. He goes willingly, hoping maybe someone can explain to him what is going on with her.

As Amy pursues all kinds of new interests and activities— everything from cross-country skiing to opera to politics—she realizes how narrow her life has been. More important, she realizes how much more there is to learn and do in the big, beautiful world. It was all there before. Why didn't she see it?

Change is the order of the day. She redecorates the master bedroom, buys new furniture for the living room, gets a new hairdo, loses twelve pounds. She even takes a few sessions with a fashion consultant who creates a whole new look for her.

After about three years of intense searching and experimenting, one day on her way to the grocery store the thought occurs to her: her life is dramatically different; she is off the plateau. She is still married to Dan; their relationship has survived the difficult times and become more intimate. She still works for the same company in the job she created. Nothing much has changed around her; she has changed. She changed in the way she experienced life. She became more than a wife, mother, and career person. She is a whole person, capable of experiencing life on a multitude of different levels. She has expanded her capacity to feel, to experience, and to just "be." The pain that instigated it was all worth it.

Confronting Your Complacency

Sometimes a plateau is a result of complacency. We don't want to do what it takes to get out. It's important, however, that we don't confuse laziness with complacency. If we tell ourselves that we have been stuck in the same boring job for years because we are just plain lazy, we are doing ourselves a disservice. The more we tell ourselves that we are defective and inadequate, the more we sink into depression about our unhappy situation. Most of us aren't lazy by any means. We spend an enormous amount of time and energy commuting to work, working, and thinking about work once we've left.

When you are in an unhappy situation, you expend a lot of negative energy for which you receive little in return.

Some of us are somewhat smug in our misery. We take a kind of grim glee in complaining about our boring situation, but we refuse to do anything about it. It's as though we are hypnotized by the mundane, routine nature of our lives. We find it hard enough to change even the simplest personal habits, such as following a strict routine every morning when we get up. So why would we want to go through the arduous task of breaking out of our plateau?

For some of us it takes a fairly dramatic event to get us off dead center. Sometimes the only thing that will motivate us is excruciating pain. We've all heard stories of people who have almost died and how their lives were transformed as a result. With a heightened appreciation of their mortality, they operate on a different level of consciousness. They fill their days with meaning instead of going through the motions of life.

That's obviously a difficult way to get rid of complacency Perhaps you can create a similar experience for yourself by contemplating and visualizing what it would be like if you died without realizing your dreams.

9

Turning Your Dreams into Reality

It is not because things are difficult that we do not dare; it is because we do not dare that they are difficult.

—*Seneca*

The dream of having a career that brings us joy and a sense of purpose is one we all have a right to fulfill. When we settle for a career that fails to call forth our greatness, that provides us with little or no opportunities for expressing our own unique talents and abilities, we cheat ourselves and the world. We are like a rich mine with all our gold left buried beneath the surface.

Finding and fulfilling your life's mission is never an easy task. It takes courage and persistence. The world usually doesn't encourage and cheer on the risk taker, the dreamer. So it is often a lonely journey. Here is how one person found his life's work and the challenges he encountered along the way.

> John Carmen has made the decision. He's packing up and checking out. His life in corporate America is soon to come to an end. Actually, he's not sure how soon because he has one major problem. He doesn't know what he wants to do. All he knows is he's going to get out.
>
> John is a bit embarrassed and bewildered over the fact that he doesn't have any dreams. Well, that's not entirely true. He has dreams for his two children. His greatest satisfaction in life has come from watching them achieve and succeed. When they came along some twenty years ago, providing for their financial security and well-being became his number one priority.

Now that goal is about to be realized, and John needs new dreams. Wistfully, he remembers how, as a young man in high school and college, he dreamed of doing great things with his life. He dreamed of a career that would enable him to leave his own unique stamp on the world, that would enable him to make a difference. But then he got swept away in a sea of responsibility and routine. He followed the crowd, got married, secured a well-paying respectable job, and had children.

Today, John can hardly remember those dreams, but he can remember the excitement he felt at the thought of the limitless possibilities. It's not that he's been particularly unhappy in his life and career all these years. His career has provided him with a comfortable, secure lifestyle; he's been able to acquire a lot of valuable skills and a wealth of experience. In the back of his mind, though, there's always been a nagging thought that he was missing something, that he was capable of more. He instinctively knows that the security afforded by his present and past employers has kept him from reaching his full potential.

Now that his family is nearly grown, he's ready to take some risks. Still middle-aged, he figures there's time for a whole new career and perhaps even a totally new lifestyle. But the questions are: "What does he really want to do?" and "What would make him supremely happy?"

John's Career Empowerment Process

Defining the Problem. John's problem is that he doesn't know what he wants to do. He has no dreams. He has a burning desire to do something different with his life, but he is having difficulty converting his desires into dreams.

Creating the Vision. Although John doesn't have a specific dream or goal in mind, he envisions a new career that would enable him to call his own shots and that would totally captivate him. He envisions himself doing something that would enable him to use all his talents, skills, and past experience.

Acknowledging and Accepting the Feelings. John must deal with the anger and sadness he feels over having neglected so many of his own dreams as a young man and as an adult. He must also struggle with his fears, particularly the fear that he may fail and lose what he has already acquired. As he strives to stop caretaking everyone else and putting their feelings first, he will have to deal with his feelings of guilt and anger.

Making Conscious Choices. John must make choices that will enable him to discover and fulfill his dream. He must choose to give himself permission to do what he wants to do with his career.

Dream or Die

Our dreams give us hope. Without hope we die—perhaps not a physical, but certainly a spiritual death. Our dreams call forth the best that is in us. They are the embryos of success, the stepping stones to satisfaction and fulfillment. They make otherwise impossible situations bearable and offer a window of escape. When we lose our dreams, we lose part of ourselves. We live our lives in black and white instead of technicolor.

> **You sink into hopelessness and despair, not because of an unbearable situation, but because you have stopped dreaming.**

John Needs a Mission

In the last year or so, John has noticed a change in himself that he doesn't like. Since his children left home, he seems to have lost some of his vitality. He doesn't take as good care of himself. He rolls out of bed in the morning as late as possible. When he arrives at the office, he goes through his daily routine as though he's on automatic. He's let his diet go, and he's cut back his gym workouts to once or twice a week. His waistline shows it.

John is beginning to think there is something to this midlife crisis business. Could it be happening to him, he wonders? He's perplexed because he's been looking forward to this period of his life for along time, when he and his wife could relax and enjoy things now that the kids were grown up.

Recently, John had lunch with one of his oldest friends, Lee Baxter, whom he hadn't seen in quite a while. Lee had started his own business a few years ago and looked like a million bucks. He was almost childlike in his enthusiasm and excitement as he spoke about his new venture. John was envious. He realized that Lee had something he didn't: he had a goal, something that excited and challenged him.

After some reflection, John decided that the "easy" life wasn't always the best life, at least not for him. He needed a purpose beyond paying the bills, buying more "things," and going on more vacations. He needed a mission that would infuse him with a passion for living. So he set about the task of finding his dream.

When You Feel You Have No Dreams

There are three kinds of people: those who have a dream and are actively pursuing it; those who have a dream but do nothing to make it come true; and those who have lost their dreams. If we are to change our careers and our lives for the better, we must take an inventory of our hopes and aspirations.

If you have lost our dreams, you need to go back and find out what happened. You need to resurrect the vision for your life or create a new one. No matter how long ago you lost it or how meaningless your life may seem today, you can still dream again.

> **Each of us was born with limitless possibilities and within those possibilities there are dreams to be dreamed, whether you believe it or not.**

Until you understand what happened, you cannot go forward. Until you can accept yourself and your past, you cannot live fully in the present, nor can you hope for the future. Here are some of the common reasons people lose their dreams. See if any of them apply to you:

▶ I sacrificed my dreams for someone else's.
▶ I didn't believe I deserved to have them come true.
▶ Life became so difficult that just surviving took all of my energy and attention.
▶ I was so terrified of failing that I never tried to fulfill my dreams.
▶ I tried to gain acceptance from others by pursuing someone else's aspirations for me rather than my own.
▶ I didn't believe I was smart enough.

> **Sometimes you have goals that you call dreams. If the goal doesn't excite you and provide your life with purpose and direction, perhaps you need to find new dreams.**

Exercise 1

Write down all the dreams you've had in your life that you gave up. Go back as far as you can remember. Beside each one, write the reason you gave it up. Be as honest as you can.

Exercise 2

Look at your lost dreams list. Put checkmarks by the ones you are sorry you gave up. Beside each of the lost dreams you would like to recapture, write down all the reasons why you think you can't, why you think it's impossible or too late. For each reason that you can't, give yourself at least three reasons why you can. Give yourself a good argument.

John Claims His Right

John is experiencing a lot of anxiety over his decision to begin a new career. He's also feeling a bit embarrassed over the fact that at age forty-five he doesn't know what he wants to do with his life. Every now and then, a little voice says, "Come on, John, you are too old to start over. You missed your chance. Don't be foolish and throw away what you have."

John's desire to experience more in life, however, is stronger than the little voice. He is determined to pursue his new course, once he decides what it is. But first he is curious to understand why he gave up his dreams in the first place. He wants to know where that little voice comes from.

Early in his career, John made the decision to give his family the very best of everything; whatever it took, that's what he would do. His two sons wanted to attend Ivy League colleges, so that became one of John's primary goals. Over the years, he passed up a number of exciting but risky career opportunities, which he didn't feel free to take because of his wife and children.

When John was a young man he gave up his dreams; he doesn't need or want to do that now. Born into a family of five children, John knew all too well the meaning of financial insecurity. His parents were constantly under pressure to make ends meet. Then, when John was fifteen, his father died of a sudden illness, leaving John, the eldest, to watch out for his younger brothers and sisters.

John was an excellent athlete in high school. One of the most disappointing days of his life was the day he passed up a football scholarship to a major university so that he could stay home and help his mother raise and support the other children. It never occurred to John, until now, that his dreams and wishes are as important as anyone else's, and he has a right to pursue them.

Now that he understands why he hasn't pursued more of his own dreams, he feels better about moving forward. He realizes it has nothing to do with his inadequacy as a person, or his character, or a lack of ability.

Discarding the Myths

Many of us give up our hopes of finding a fulfilling career because we buy a truckload of myths—myths that we still believe today.

> **Until you challenge the myths and develop your own set of beliefs based on truth, you can never fulfill your dreams.**

Here are some of the popular myths that stand in the way of our dreams:

Myth 1: Work is not supposed to be fun. Some of us think that, if we aren't struggling and sacrificing, we aren't working. Work may be a four-letter word to us because we never had role models show us that work can and should be enjoyable. We may not dream about finding satisfaction and fulfillment in our work because on a deep level we may not believe it is attainable.

Myth 2: Work should come before everything else. If we saw our parents or others who were significant in our lives put work first at all times, we may find ourselves doing the same. We may have an overdeveloped sense of responsibility when it comes to work, particularly if we look for it to give us our sense of self-esteem. Certainly there are times when our career should come first, but when it's always the number one priority we pay a high price. Our career dreams may eventually turn our lives into a nightmare because we have sacrificed everything.

Myth 3: Above all else, we should seek a career that provides us with financial success. It's hard to achieve our dreams when we are blinded by dollar signs. If we were encouraged to pursue only high-paying professions, we may have missed our calling. If we saw our role models live in fear of not having enough money, we may not take the financial gamble required to pursue a new line of work, even though we earnestly desire it and are perfectly suited for it.

Myth 4: If you're a woman, it isn't important to achieve career success. If women are taught that a woman's place is in the home, that a woman needed to marry success instead of achieve it on her own, they may use only a small fraction of their potential. If no one along the way believed in them and encouraged them to achieve great things, they may set their sights too low.

Myth 5: You are a success in life, if you are a success in your career. If our only criterion for a successful life is success at work, then we usually wind up living a lopsided life. It's difficult to find satisfaction and fulfillment in life when we ignore our basic needs.

Exercise 1

Write down the myths that you were taught while growing up and that have affected where you are in your career today. For each myth, write yourself a new message that is self-affirming and based on the truth. Read the new messages at least five times each day until you believe them.

John Examines His Beliefs

John grew up with a lot of mistaken ideas about work, which have affected the career decisions he made over the years. If he wants to embark on a whole new endeavor, John realizes he needs to reexamine some of those ideas and beliefs.

He sees other people having fun in their work, but sometimes he has difficulty believing that it could be that much fun for him. When he was a child, "work" was what made his mother and father so tired that they rarely had any energy for him. He watched his parents work to the point of exhaustion just to put food on the table. His father worked as a brick layer while his mother worked cleaning homes for people. Rarely did they talk about getting any satisfaction from their work. Most of John's friends' parents did similar types of work. So in his early years, he never thought of work as something one did for reasons other than to survive.

John also grew up believing that he had to make a lot of money to be a success. John's parents wanted a better life for him, so they put a lot of pressure on him to get an education and pursue a career that would, first and foremost, provide abundant financial rewards. Whenever he talked about what he wanted to be when he grew up, the comment usually was, "They don't make enough money. Why don't you do something else?"

John also got the message that, if you are a success in your job, you are a success in life. He knows his parents often felt inferior around people who had more money and more prestigious jobs. Whenever John brought someone home to visit, particularly a girlfriend, the first thing they wanted to know was what her parents did for a living. John came to believe at a young age that anyone who lived in a nice house, earned a lot of money, and had a good, steady, respectable job was a success at life. They had no reason to feel ashamed. When John achieved all those things and still felt something was missing, he began to question his belief.

When Your Dreams Are Not Your Own

When we're born, people often have aspirations for us. They dream of our accomplishing great things, doing what they never had the opportunity to do. Although they may be well-intended, there is an inherent problem. If they dream too much for us, we may lose the capacity to dream for ourselves. In our effort to please and gain their acceptance, we take on their hopes for us as our own. We become lawyers when we would rather be schoolteachers.

> **Other people may give you goals but they cannot give you dreams. A goal is something to be achieved. A dream is a goal impassioned with love and desire.**

No one else can give you the desires of your own heart; those must be discovered on your own. Here are some questions to help you determine if you're living your own dream or someone else's dream for you.

	Yes	No
1. Did someone else convince you to pursue a certain line of work?	❑	❑

	Yes	No
2. Do you find yourself fantasizing about doing something totally different from what you are doing now?	❏	❏
3. Is your job simply a way of earning a living and nothing more?	❏	❏
4. Are you bored by your work?	❏	❏
5. Did you choose a career because that's what a parent or other relative chose?	❏	❏
6. Do you feel your job provides you with little or no opportunity to express yourself and your uniqueness?	❏	❏
7. Were you criticized growing up for wanting to pursue a line of work that others thought was unacceptable?	❏	❏
8. Do you feel guilty because you're not more committed to your work?	❏	❏
9. Do you feel trapped by the financial security and perks provided by your current job?	❏	❏

John Looks at His Choices

As John answers the questions in the previous section, there is no doubt in his mind. He has pursued a career to satisfy someone else's desires for him rather than his own.

His mother insisted that he major in business in college. He had little interest in pursuing a business career; he thought he would much prefer doing something outside, like working with nature in some way or coaching football. His mother, however, wouldn't hear of it. Every time he talked about what he wanted to be, she criticized his ideas. John had seen his mother sacrifice so much for him and his brothers and sisters over the years that he didn't have the heart to disappoint her. And that is how he ended up as a partner in a large accounting firm.

In the early years of his career, John didn't spend a lot of time thinking about what he would rather do. He concentrated on getting ahead and making money to support his family. In recent years, though, he has found himself daydreaming more and more at work about doing something different with his life and career. His fantasies seem to be filling an ever-increasing void.

John likes the people with whom he works; that's where he has derived most of his satisfaction. He particularly enjoys working with the young people coming up in the organization, helping them to grow and develop. Otherwise, he has no great love or interest in what he does.

John doesn't feel particularly creative in his work, which is one of the problems. He's actually surprised that he's been able to achieve as much as he has in his career, considering his lack of genuine interest in the field.

John has always performed well and pulled his share. Sometimes, though, as a partner, he feels he should be more enthusiastic and committed; he just can't get himself to eat and breathe the business.

John does, however, enjoy the financial security and perks provided by the job. Sometimes he thinks that is the only reason he has stayed in the field all these years.

Forgiving Ourselves and Others

Anger and resentment are the enemies of our dreams. As long as we blame someone else for taking our dreams away from us or blame ourselves for allowing them to do so, we stay stuck in our own misery. If we berate ourselves for being too weak, too lazy, too scared, too incompetent—whatever stick we beat ourselves up with—we do ourselves a disservice. We need to remind ourselves often that in the past we did the best we could at the time. If we could have done differently, we would have. The people in our past who may have hurt us also did the best they could at the time, even though it may seem that it wasn't good enough.

> **When you give up your dreams it's always because you are hurt and afraid—not because you are weak and defective.**

Exercise 1

If you feel bad about not fulfilling your dreams, write yourself a letter of forgiveness. Write the letter as though you are writing to your best friend. In the letter, tell yourself that you understand why you let your dreams die and that it's OK. Tell yourself all the reasons that you deserve to have your dreams come true now and why it's not too late.

Exercise 2

If you are angry at another person—such as a parent or spouse—who you feel has hindered you in fulfilling your dreams, write them a letter of forgiveness. Tell them that you understand why they did what they did and that you no longer hold them accountable. Tell them you are taking responsibility for your own life and your own career happiness.

John Lets Go of the Past

John is somewhat angry and resentful that it's taken him forty-five years to feel free enough to have his own dreams and pursue them. He doesn't regret having helped his brothers and sisters or having provided well for his children. He feels good about what he was able to give them. What he doesn't feel good about is the way he almost totally neglected himself in the process. He asks himself why it had to be so one-sided. Why couldn't the others have made some compromises so that he could have realized more of his dreams as well?

John is mostly mad at himself. He realizes that he chose to pass up the football scholarship. He chose to sacrifice his own career dreams so that his children could achieve theirs. Sometimes he thinks he made those choices so that he wouldn't have to risk failure himself. Or perhaps he did not pursue his dreams because of low self-esteem, because he thought other people were more important than he. Or was it because he had such a strong need to be needed? When others depended on him, he had a sense of importance.

His mother was always telling him she didn't think she could survive without him. She constantly told him how proud his father would be of him. When it came time for him to go to college, she didn't tell him he couldn't take the scholarship, but she didn't encourage him either. She kept telling him that she thought he should live at home and go to the local junior college. Part of him blames her for his career path.

John knows that he can't afford to use up valuable energy on resentments about the past. Even though his mother is dead, he writes her a letter telling her that he understands why she tried to hold onto him for so long. In the letter, he tells her he no longer holds her accountable; he's taking responsibility for *his own happiness. One of the ways he's doing so is by pursuing a new career—one that he has chosen.*

The Key to Our Dreams

If you are still perplexed about what to do with your career, if you still don't have a star to hitch your wagon to, start with your talents and gifts. The gifts we were given are intended for use.

Some of us know ourselves well. We know what we're good at and what we have no aptitude for. Others of us are like a reservoir of untapped resources. We don't even know what's inside. Here are some questions to help you find work that is uniquely yours:

▶ When are you the happiest?
▶ What kinds of activities do you enjoy most?
▶ What kinds of things were you good at in school?
▶ What was the most satisfying job you ever had and why?
▶ What are your hobbies?
▶ What achievements in your life are you most proud of?
▶ What can you do better than anyone you know?
▶ If you were granted one wish, that you could be whatever you wanted to be, what would you wish?

> **When you fully use your gifts and talents in your work, you make a profound expression of who you are.**

John Takes an Inventory

John has the advantage of knowing what he likes and where his talents and strengths lie. He wants to embark on something totally new and different without throwing away all his years of valuable experience. How will he find a new career that will be challenging and exciting, that will utilize his talents and past experiences to the fullest, and that will enable him to earn a decent living?

Instead of trying to answer the question, "What do I want to do?" John first looks backwards and inward. He decides he's happiest when he is outdoors and doing something physical. This gives him a starting place.

John has always enjoyed sports. He still plays a mean game of tennis and has run three marathons in the past eight years. As his children were growing up, John coached Little League. One of his proudest accomplishments was taking his youngest son's baseball team to the state championship. Every year, he helps with the Special Olympics, which gives him a lot of satisfaction.

In high school, John was the senior class president and captain of the football team. Even in his accounting firm, people look to him for leadership. John knows he has a real gift for winning peoples' trust. He is also an outstanding public speaker. In his work, he's often asked to speak at trade association meetings because he knows the field so well and can entertain a crowd.

He likes working with his hands. When he was in high school, he had a talent for woodworking. He has a shop at home where he makes all kinds of small furniture items such as desks, wooden stools, tables, and lamps.

By the time John finished doing an inventory of his talents, skills, and interests, he was impressed with himself. He realized he was much more than an accountant.

More Ways to Discover Our Dreams

Some of us had the luxury of knowing at a very young age what we wanted to be when we grew up. Some of us may still be waiting to find out. We may envy those on a clear straight path, who love what they do. Why can't we find our own special niche in life?

If you find yourself in such a position, it simply means you have more exploring to do. You need to find out more about yourself and the opportunities out there for you. Here are some suggestions:

▶ Talk to other people about what they do.
▶ Strike up conversations with strangers. Ask them specific questions about their work: what exactly do they do, why do they do it, why do they like it, how did they get into the field?
▶ Read, read, read. Read about other people and what they do. Read trade journals for the field you may be interested in.
▶ Take some courses. If you think you may be interested in another field, take a course at a local college.
▶ Volunteer. If you're interested in a field that utilizes volunteers, by all means get involved. Perhaps you want to work with handicapped children. What better way to find out than by working on a volunteer basis?

▶ Ask people you know if you can observe them at work. For example, if you think you might want to be a stockbroker, ask a stockbroker you know if you can shadow him or her, for a day.

▶ Keep your mind open and don't rule out anything. You may find your niche in the most unexpected place.

People bloom at different stages of life. It is no disgrace at any age not to have found work that brings you satisfaction and fulfillment. What matters is that you search until you find it.

John Investigates an Idea

After doing an extensive inventory of his talents, skills, experience, and interests, John's dream begins to take shape. As John goes over his inventory and reflects on when he is the happiest, one idea keeps coming up for him: to open a camp. The first time he thought of it, he was riding down the street in his Jeep in a wealthy section of town when he spotted a group of teenagers hanging out on the street corner. Despite their apparent affluence, they had the same empty sad looks you might see on the faces of kids in the ghetto.

Although he doesn't know much about it, the thought of opening a camp for kids excites John for a number of reasons. He would be working with young people, which he enjoys doing. It would fit perfectly with his love of the outdoors and sports. He could even utilize his woodworking skills. Owning and running a camp would require a tremendous amount of leadership ability and management skills; John is a pro at both. His accounting background and business consulting will provide him with the knowledge and experience needed to run a successful business. He could even use his public speaking skills in promoting the camp.

The more he thinks about the idea, the more he likes it, but he knows he needs to do in-depth research and investigation. Does he want it to be a special interest camp? If so, what kind? Should it be for problem kids or for all kids? Should it be a low-cost camp for underprivileged kids or a posh camp for wealthy children?

*And, of course, the big questions are, "What would the cap-
ital investment be? How much would it cost to operate?"
Maybe he could buy a camp with a partner, or perhaps a group
of backers, and he could run it.*

*John leaves his mind completely open as he goes about his
investigation. Even at this stage, he realizes that a camp may
not be what he wants to do or may not be feasible. He won't
know until he asks the right questions of the right people. Here
are some of the steps John takes:*

◗ *Go to the public library to research the subject of camps.
Do a computer search of newspaper and magazine arti-
cles published on the subject over the past few years.
Check to see if there are trade journals on camps or recreation for kids.*
◗ *Find out where to obtain a directory of camps by state.*
◗ *Using the directory, write away to carious types of camps
to obtain brochures and information.*
◗ *Set up exploratory meetings with owners/ managers of
camps.*
◗ *Talk to the head of the Recreation Department at the
nearest college. Ask him or her for other sources of
information.*

*As John goes about his research, each person he meets directs
him to additional sources of information. His search soon begins
to feel like a scavenger hunt. Each question leads to another
question, which in the beginning he didn't even know to ask.*

The Dream Invaders

Once we have found our dream and are on a course, many
forces try to convince us that we are pursuing the impossible, that
we should give up. If we know we will encounter them before
beginning, we can prepare ourselves. We won't be as upset by
them because we know they are just part of the experience of
pursuing a dream. Here are ten of the best ways to invade or kill
a dream:

1. Give other people's opinions and beliefs more credence than
you give your own.

2. Take on other people's fears. If a spouse, parent, or friend is afraid of the risk you are taking, let their feelings dampen your enthusiasm.

3. Give up when you encounter an obstacle. The road to your dreams will be paved with stumbling blocks. If you let them defeat you, they will.

4. Think negatively. Nothing will stifle a dream faster than negative thoughts.

5. Fail to take care of yourself. If you exhaust yourself in the early stages of your pursuit, you may not have enough energy and stamina for the rest of the race. Pace yourself.

6. Be harsh on yourself. When you are pursuing anything you've never done before, you are bound to make mistakes. If you are unmerciful with yourself when you mess up, you will be using up valuable energy that could be put toward your dream.

7. Be rigid and inflexible. If you see things as black and white and in absolutes you may miss some great opportunities. If you don't allow your dream to change its shape as you go along, it may die.

8. Fail to plan. If you don't do the necessary planning in advance, your dream will remain a wish rather than a reality.

9. Expect results overnight. If you are impatient, you may give up if you don't see immediate results. Big dreams are usually a long time in the making.

10. Fail to make a commitment. Commitment is a dream in action. A commitment enables you to push forward when all looks bleak, when it looks like you should give up. Commitment gives you staying power.

John Pushes Forward

John wishes his friends and family would share some of his enthusiasm and offer just a little support. Instead, most of them keep telling him why it won't work. He has two friends who are cheering him on, but the rest think he has lost some screws. The standard response goes something like this: "But you don't know anything about running a camp." "I don't think there's much money in it." "What do you want to do that for?"

Some of the people who have responded negatively are successful business people whom he respects. Their comments have caused him to doubt himself and to wonder if he is chasing a pipedream. Maybe he should let the idea remain a fantasy. Then he looks at how most of them have led their lives—in a very safe, conventional manner. Naturally, they wouldn't be able to conceive of someone making such a bold move—except for one friend who secretly admits that he too would like to do something different but doesn't have the guts.

John decides to listen to others' opinions but is determined not to let them make his decision for him. After all, most great endeavors in the beginning are usually looked upon with skepticism. He resolves to let the facts and his own intuitive sense guide him rather than the opinions of other people.

John can deal with his friends. But he has much more difficulty with his wife Andrea's lack of support. Not only doesn't she support him, she is strongly opposed to the idea. This is a tough one for John because, throughout his life, he has always sacrificed his wishes for the wishes of those closest to him. Andrea can't understand why at this point in their lives he would want to make such a drastic change. Why would he want to risk what they have worked so hard for? He has a good job that provides them with a very comfortable way of life. They have a beautiful home and, now that the children are grown, they are free to travel and come and go as they please. "What could be better?" she asks. Andrea tells him she thinks he is being unfair; she thinks she has earned the right to take things easier.

As he listens to her pleading, John almost gives up. The more he thinks about it, though, the angrier he becomes. He is angry because she has made assumptions about what will happen without having all the facts. She doesn't seem to care whether he is happy in what he is doing.

A close friend of theirs from high school reminds John that Andrea grew up in a poor family with little or no security. So naturally she doesn't want to risk what she has. She is probably reacting out of fear.

John is determined to pursue his dream; he too feels he has earned the right to do what he wants at this stage of his life. He's sensitive to Andrea's concerns, though, and does everything he can to relieve her fears. Together they developed some guidelines and parameters for the venture: how much money they will risk, alternative plans if the project doesn't work out, and what, if any, responsibilities Andrea will have to the project.

Imaging Your Dream

The more focused your dream, the greater the chances are that you will achieve it. We need to have a mental picture of what it will be like when our dream comes true. Like Don Quixote, we need to have a vision.

Your mental picture can keep the dream alive, particularly when your thoughts and feelings start to tell you that it's not worth it, that it's unattainable.

Exercise 1

Take a plain piece of paper and some color crayons, old magazines, and glue. Make a picture of yourself having fulfilled your dream. Let yourself go and be creative. Forget about whether you have any artistic ability. The idea is to get out of your left brain and into your right brain. In other words, let your imagination soar. As you make the picture, be as detailed as you can. Let your picture express the emotions you think you will feel.

Exercise 2

Take five minutes out of every day to do nothing but visualize your dream. Look at your picture and then close your eyes. See yourself achieving it.

John Has a Vision

John's dream is now crystal clear. He can envision it in his mind's eye. He's going to start a camp for problem teenagers. It will be designed for kids from middle-class homes who are displaying behavioral problems but who haven't become chemically dependent or criminal. It won't be just recreational. Campers will learn skills for living. In addition to the regular camp activities, they will learn things such as how to handle money, how to resolve conflict with other people, how to get along with their families, and how to appropriately express feelings.

John's vision was of a group of boys playing touch football in an open meadow on a bright, summer day. The game is in play and John is on the sidelines encouraging one of the kids who is having difficulty participating. At the other end of the meadow, the girls are playing softball while the camp chefs prepare a barbecue nearby. The hamburgers are stacked a mile high beside the grill, and the watermelons are being unloaded from the truck.

John has the picture indelibly stamped in his mind. Each morning, he closes his eyes and pulls up the image in his mind. He tries to smell the smells, feel the sun on his face, and hear the sounds of laughter. Whenever he begins to feel discouraged or impatient, he takes a few minutes by himself and recalls the image.

Conclusion

If someone were to ask us how we got to where we are in life, many of us would be hard-pressed to give an explanation. Our lives are like a play. We stumble onto the stage with a script that someone else wrote for us and we act it out.

Instead of being the stars, producers, and directors of our plays, we sometimes settle for being actors, and not very good ones. At least good actors bring their true, authentic selves to their roles. We go through the scenes of our lives almost unconsciously; we let other people—parents, employers, spouses—direct us according to their values, beliefs, and rules. We become what we think they want us to be. We give away our power and then we wonder why we don't like the play. We don't like our characters, the story lines, the sets, the other characters, anything about it.

Some of us cope by looking for new roles in new plays. We find new jobs or get new spouses or move to new cities. But sooner or later we find ourselves in the same place. If we are to find true satisfaction and fulfillment in our lives and careers, we must become the directors and producers. We must do more than act out roles. We must take our power back.

Like the characters we visited, we take our power back by defining the problem(s) and owning our parts in it, by creating a vision of how we would like it to be, by acknowledging and accepting our feelings, and by making conscious choices.

When we take back our power—when we change from actors to directors—we turn our lives around. We call our own shots. Now the play is filled with richness and passion; it is truly an art form. What others think of our play is no longer of all-consuming importance; it satisfies us and that is enough. Because we are true to ourselves and in control of our own destinies, we are able to take the risks necessary to achieve our dreams.

We become victims or victors in life by the choices we make. If we feel victimized, if our jobs are not giving us the satisfaction we desire, it is up to us to turn our situations around. No one else can do it for us.

Realizing our career visions requires hard work, courage, and risk taking. We must challenge our old values, beliefs, and ways of doing things. We must leave what is safe and familiar behind.

The process is usually painful and filled with confusion, but well worth the effort. When we find our life's work, we come home to ourselves. We are able to more fully express who we are. We feel that our lives count and make a difference in the world.

If you have committed yourself to creating the kind of career you've always dreamed of, I congratulate you and hope you have found within this book some useful tools for the journey. Good luck!

Bibliography

Career Development

Adams, James. L. *Conceptual Blockbusting: A Guide to Better Ideas.* 3rd ed. Reading, Mass.: Addison-Wesley Publishing Company, 1990.

Arnold, John D. *When the Sparks Fly: Resolving Conflicts in Your Organization.* New York: McGraw-Hill, 1992.

Arrendondo, Lani. *How to Present Like a Pro: Getting People to See Things Your Way.* New York: McGraw-Hill, 1991.

Banville, Thomas G. How to Listen—*How to Be Heard.* Chicago: Nelson-Hall, 1978.

Bardwick, Judith M., Ph.D. *The Plateauing Trap: How to Avoid It in Your Career and in Your Life.* New York: AMACOM, 1986.

Berne, Eric. *What Do You Say After You Say Hello?* New York: Bantam Books, 1984.

Bernstein, Albert J. *Dinosaur Brains: Dealing with All Those Impossible People at Work.* New York: Ballantine Books, 1990.

Block, Peter. *The Empowered Manager: Positive Political Skills at Work.* San Francisco: Jossey-Bass, 1991.

Blohowiak, Donald W. *Mavericks.* Homewood, Ill.: Business One Irwin, 1992.

Boe, Anne and Bette B. Youngs. *Is Your "Net" Working? A Complete Guide to Building Contacts and Career Visibility.* New York: John Wiley & Sons, 1989.

Bolles, Richard N. *The Three Boxes of Life and How to Get Out of Them.* Berkeley, Calif.: Ten Speed Press, 1981.

Bones, Richard N. *What Color Is Your Parachute?* Berkeley, Calif.: Ten Speed Press, 1992.

Chusmir, Leonard H. *Thank God It's Monday: The Guide to a Happier Job.* New York: NAL-Dutton,1990.

Cohen, Allan R. and David Bradford. *Influence Without Authority.* New York: John Wiley & Sons, 1991.

Covey, Stephen. *Principle Centered Leadership.* New York: Simon & Schuster, 1990.

Covey, Stephen. *Seven Habits of Highly Successful People*. New York: Simon & Schuster Trade, 1989.

Davidson, Jeffrey P. *Blow Your Own Horn: How to Get Noticed and Get Ahead*. New York: Berkley Publishing Group, 1991.

Deep, Sam and Lyle Sussman. *Smart Moves*. Reading, Mass.: Addison-Wesley, 1990.

Dilenschneider, Robert. *Power and Influence: Mastering the Art of Persuasion*. New York: Prentice Hall, 1991.

Douglass, Merrill E. and Donna N. Douglass. *Manage Your Time, Manage Your Work, Manage Yourself*. New York: AMACOM, 1985.

Fisher, Roger and William Ury. *Getting to Yes: Negotiating Agreement Without Giving In*, rev ed. New York: Viking Penguin, 1991.

Gale, Barry and Linda. *Stay or Leave—A Complete System to Decide Whether to Remain at Your Job or Pack Your Travelling Bag*. New York: Harper & Row, 1989.

Hathaway, Patti and Susan D. Schubert. *Managing Upward: Strategies For Succeeding with Your Boss*. Los Altos, Calif.: Crisp Publications, 1992.

Hyatt, Carole. *Shifting Gears—How to Master Career Change and Find the Work That's for You*. New York: Simon & Schuster, 1990.

Johnson, Spencer. *Yes or No: The Guide to Better Decisions—A Story*. New York: Harper Business, 1992.

Koestenbaum, Peter. *Leadership: The Inner Side of Greatness*. San Francisco: Jossey-Bass, 1991.

McGee-Cooper, Ann, with Duane Trammell and Barbara Lau. *You Don't Have to Go Home from Work Exhausted! The Energy Engineering Approach*. Dallas: Bowen and Rogers Publishing Company, 1990.

Piumez, Jacqueline Hornor, with Dougherty, Karia. *Divorcing a Corporation*. New York: Villiard Books, 1986.

Ryan, Kathleen D. and Daniel K. Oestreich. *Driving Fear out of the Workplace: How to Overcome the Invisible Barriers to Quality, Productivity and Innovation*. San Francisco: Jossey-Bass, 1991.

Sinetar, Marsha. *Do What You Love, The Money Will Follow*. New York: Dell Publishing, 1987.

Straat, Kent L. *What Your Boss Can't Tell You*. New York: AMACOM, 1988.

"Survey Shows Growing Job Malaise Despite Boom Times in U.S. Labor Market." *BNA Daily Labor Report*, October 17, 2000.

Von Oech, Roger, Ph.D. *A Whack on the Side of the Head: How to Unlock Your Mind for Innovation*, rev ed. New York: Warner Books, 1990.

Walther, George R. *Power Talking: Fifty Ways to Say What You Mean and Get What You Want*. New York: Putnam Publishing Group, 1991.

Walton, Richard E. *Managing Conflict: Interpersonal Dialogue and Third Party Roles*. Reading, Mass.: Addison-Wesley, 1987.

Zuker, Elaina. *Seven Secrets of Influence*. New York: McGraw-Hill, 1991.

Personal Growth and Healing

Ackerman, Robert J., Ph.D. *Perfect Daughters*. Deerfield Beach, Fla.: Health Communications, 1989.

Beattie, Melody. *Codependent No More: How to Stop Controlling Others and Start Caring for Yourself*. San Francisco: Harper/Hazelden, 1987.

Bradshaw, John. *The Family*. Deerfield Beach, Fla.: Health Communications, 1988.

Corbin, Carolyn, with Gene Busnar. *Conquering Corporate Codependent Life Skills for Making It Within and Without the Corporation*. Prentice Hall: Englewood Cliffs, N.J., 1993.

Gawain, Shakti. *Creative Visualization*. San Raphael, Calif.: New World Library, 1978.

Johnson, Anthony Godby. *A Rock and a Hard Place*. New York: Crown Publishers, 1993.

La Bier, Douglas. *Modern Madness: The Emotional Fallout of Success*. Reading, Mass.: Addison-Wesley, 1986.

Lerner, Harriet Goidhor. *Dance of Anger*. New York: Harper & Row, 1985.

Moore, Thomas. *Care of the Soul. A Guide for Cultivating Depth and Sacredness in Every Day Life*. New York: Harper Collins, 1992.

Peck, M. Scott. *The Road Less Traveled*. New York: Touchstone/ Simon & Schuster, 1978.

Riley, Mary, Ph.D. *Corporate Healing*. Deerfield Beach, Fla.: Health Communications, 1990.

Scheaf, Anne Wilson. *Women's Reality: How You Can Realize Your Full Potential*. New York: Harper Paperbacks, 1985.

Steinem, Gloria. *Revolution from Within: A Book of Self Esteem*. Boston: Little Brown, 1992.

About the Author

Diane Tracy is a coach to executives in Fortune 500 companies. She also speaks before thousands of people each year in the course of conducting workshops and seminars for companies and organizations. Her clients include MTV, AT&T, the United Nations, HBO, Philips Electronics, Bristol-Myers Squibb, and the Social Security Administration. Ms. Tracy has appeared on more than 150 radio and television talks shows and is the author of *Truth, Trust and the Bottom Line, 10 Steps to Empowerment,* and *The First Book of Common-Sense Management.*